ENCH ... ED
JOURNEYS

Guided
Meditations
for Magical
Transformation

SARAH ROBINSON

WOMANCRAFT PUBLISHING

Medical Disclaimer

Meditation is a beautiful tool, but it is not a cure-all. If you are experiencing extremes of feeling such as depression, anxiety, severe stress and/or grief please do consider also seeking professional help such as from a counsellor or therapist to assist you in your healing journey.

Published by Womancraft Publishing, 2023
www.womancraftpublishing.com

ISBN 978-1-910559-86-4

Enchanted Journeys is also available in ebook format:
ISBN 978-1-910559-85-7

Cover design, interior design and typesetting: lucentword.com
Cover image © Izumi Omori
Continuous line images: AVA Bitter, Lilith E, Simple Line, StocKNick, Valenty, Yanina Nosova/all Shutterstock.com

Womancraft Publishing is committed to sharing powerful new women's voices, through a collaborative publishing process. We are proud to midwife this work, however the story, the experiences and the words are the authors' alone. A percentage of Womancraft Publishing profits are invested back into the environment reforesting the tropics (via TreeSisters) and forward into the community.

Praise for
Sarah Robinson

Sarah is now a trusted resource in my empowering library.

Alice Grist, *Dirty & Divine* and *The Book of Tarot*

Sarah Robinson's skillful teaching and writing encourages us to remember what we may have lost when approaching the yoga mat: the importance of stillness, of the mind-body connection, of our intentions to slow down in our fast-paced lives. It's a vital addition to anyone seeking stillness in a constantly moving world.

Sarah Justice, co-editor of *Witchology* magazine and owner of The Tiny Cauldron

Sarah Robinson continues her engaging explorations of Witchcraft, old and new…with delicious tidbits, tales and insights to nourish your craft and your spirit.

Phyllis Curott, author of *The Witches' Wisdom Tarot* and *Book of Shadows*

Acknowledgment

In naming this book we sought suggestions from our wonderful community of Womancraft readers and supporters. We extend our heartfelt gratitude for the beautiful words contributed by Toni Rakke, Katrina Rae and Sam Chandler.

Other Books by Sarah Robinson

Yoga for Witches

Yin Magic

Kitchen Witch: Food, Folklore and Fairy Tale

The Kitchen Witch Companion: Recipes, Rituals and Reflections

Contents

JOURNEYING WITH THE ELEMENTS

Introduction

Welcome! I'm so glad you're here.

For over a decade I have led meditation groups and shared recorded and live meditations online. I have witnessed the simple yet powerful magic that can be found within meditation and the healing this path can offer. Meditation can help us let go of stress and busy thoughts, it can also help us nurture and nourish ideas, intuition, empowerment, gratitude, calm and peace.

This book was born of a regularly-made request to create a book collection of the meditations that I have created over the many years of my teaching journey. Some of you may well have heard these meditations from me in my classes, via my YouTube channel or through meditation apps. The meditations I have gathered are predominantly guided visualisations, what I sometimes call 'story journeys'.

You will see through these meditations my own personal areas of passion and specialism – goddesses, folklore and myth – as strong themes. I have been inspired by all manner of deities, places and people. You'll find meditations for many occasions, for group or personal work, seasons, times of day, nature and the elements, various deities, and simply some of my personal favourites. Some are short and sweet introductions to your day, whilst others invite you to take longer journeys into the realms of intuition, deep knowing and the subconscious.

The Magic of Meditation

"Magic teaches us that things that seem to be impossible can become possible. Things that have become separated, blocked or broken, like people and energy, can be re-joined. We can find the light, find space and empty cauldrons can be refilled with time and love."

I wrote these words for my second book, *Yin Magic*, and I believe the exact same words apply to meditation as well.

There are so many reasons to meditate, not least the connection to a certain magic when we cultivate a regular meditation practice. Any time spent in stillness can be an opportunity for meditation and reflection, both on one's self and the world. Great transformation can happen in these moments, like in a chrysalis, before something new and beautiful emerges. Every moment of stillness is an opportunity to learn and grow. Taking time to observe and notice your thoughts can help you nurture a more profound sense of presence and well-being. A regular meditation practice teaches you to be able to observe and accept any thoughts and emotions that arise without judgement.

In the story of yoga, the union that is yoga can only happen when the mind becomes quiet – which is essentially what meditation is. Mental stillness is found by bringing the body, mind and senses to calm, which, in turn, relaxes the nervous system. Meditation is used to focus the mind and enter a state of consciousness different from our daily awareness. Meditation can be used to contemplate something affecting us inwardly or outwardly. During this altered state of consciousness, you may feel you can contact your inner self or communicate with the Divine/Universe/Spirit.

While meditation is more commonly associated with yoga and Eastern religions, it is also a core part of magical practice. It is the starting point for other techniques and practices such as astral projection, prayer, manifestation, shamanism and 'hedge riding'.

Meditation can be an addition to whatever healing modality you are using, a companion you can call on at any time: it is indeed a powerful magic.

How to Meditate

This is a question I get asked lot! I know that those who ask are often looking for magical words of wisdom to reveal how to do meditation. The answer may surprise you: you already know. We all already know. But we have forgotten, perhaps, the wisdom that just because something is very *simple* – which the essence of meditation is – does not mean it is *easy*.

Meditation is no more or less than dedicated focus – be that regulated attention on the breath or visual imagery or the sensations of the body. You can do meditation lying down, seated, or moving – while walking or doing tai chi. There are many forms of meditation, with similar practices spanning cultures – such as meditation to empty the mind completely of thoughts or to notice all sensations and emotions that arise without judgement. In this book I will be focusing on guided visualisations.

Meditation can be different each and every time: sometimes you may feel completely held in the experience, sometimes you may find yourself distracted and unable to settle. Try to be patient and practice non-judgement. This is a journey, it does not have to be 'perfect'.

Preparing for Meditation

o Turn off your phone, the TV, and bright lights. Make sure you are warm and comfortable.

o Bolsters, blocks, blankets and eye pillows can all be useful, but nothing is essential.

o Incense, candles and gentle music can all help you create a space that feels special and sacred, a little removed from day-to-day life.

o You may want to have a notebook and pen nearby before you begin, so that it is on hand if needed.

o Give yourself time and space to settle physically and mentally at the beginning of the meditation. Do not rush this part of the process.

Guidance for Leading Groups in Meditation

○ Ensure you read through the meditation alone in preparation, checking the pronunciation of any unfamiliar words (you will find these in the footnotes).

○ Before starting the meditation, centre yourself, relax your body and ensure you are breathing deeply.

○ Allow your voice to transmit a sense of ease and calm. Remember the words you are reading are an aid to meditation, so find the balance between being clearly heard (especially if there is also music playing) and yet not dominating your students' inner experience.

○ Take your time, give chances to pause and reflect at both the beginning and end of the meditation, and be sure to allow quiet moments to visualise if guided to do so.

○ As with retelling fairy tales over centuries, as you read aloud these stories, you become their carrier and they become your own! Do not worry about changing words: the energy and intention of the reading is what is most important.

○ You may want to use a singing bowl, bell or gentle chime to help signify when the meditation is coming to an end.

Writing and Journaling

Writing is a beautiful way that we can create simple and amazing magic – taking our thoughts from mind to page. It doesn't have to be great poetry or prose; it doesn't have to be for anyone but yourself. Writing can be cleansing, enriching, and grounding. It allows us to process the emotions and experiences of our life, creating reminders of times when you have achieved great things, learned new things and encountered wonder. We are creating, in writing, visual representations of what we've survived and thrived through, and a permanent record of our insights and realisations.

The ways to incorporate writing into your magical and spiritual practices are endless: writing as a form of manifesting, reflections, ritual, reminders…

The practice of journal writing dates back to the days when our ancestors wrote on cave walls, making sense of our world by recording it. A journal can play many roles: a tool for self-expression, clarity, creativity, and an exploration of what you think and feel. For something so simple, there are a fantastic number of benefits linked to journaling from calming anxiety and stress to increasing mental clarity, creativity, awareness and spiritual growth.

Journaling is a tool that yogis might liken to *svadhyaya* or self-study. Your journal, like your meditation time, can be a sanctuary, and place of reflection. As you look over what you are writing take time to reflect: are you holding onto anger or frustrations? Are you blaming others? Are you missing solutions that are available to you?

Meditation and Journaling: Combining Practices

By exploring your inner world through meditation and journaling, you can utilise both practices for deeper reflection and connection. Both meditation and journaling create a space for exploration: you are not trying to change or criticise, but just to observe and note thoughts and feelings as they arise. Something that we tend to have real difficulty with in modern life is stopping, reflecting or meditating: taking time to do nothing. It is easy to forget the value of doing nothing. Finding that space and silence is essential. It's only in quieting the body and mind that you allow space for inspiration, growth and relaxation. Taking time for yourself to pause from the busyness of the outer world allows you to explore, discover and learn from your inner world.

When you put thoughts to paper in your journal, you can clear your mind and gain perspective. By combining meditation and journaling, you can access deeper wisdom and cultivate a greater understanding of your experiences and what you can learn from them.

How to Use This Book

Whether using this book to lead a group or for your own personal practice, each journey will invite you to access your own deep inner knowing and connection. They are perfect for reading aloud with a circle, coven or yoga class. Or, you may wish to record the meditation and then listen to it together. If you've chosen this book for your own personal journey you can record yourself reading the meditation, or feel free to listen to me! (Details of links can all be found at my website: sentiayoga.com, this will guide you to my YouTube Channel and Insight Timer profile for a wealth of audio recordings, as well as any live-streamed events that may be coming up.)

The meditations in this book include themes of:

○   Passages and cycles of time.

○   Journeying with the divine in many forms: feminine and masculine, as well as sacred spaces.

○   The magic of the elements.

Each section includes a few questions for reflection, as well as some ideas for journaling, inviting you to spend time in deeper contemplation of your experience. If you are part of a group, the questions may be offered as points for discussion or sharing.

You do not have to follow the meditations as they are laid out in this book, especially if you are seeking a specific theme such as a meditation for the morning or a season. You can make any time of day, month or season sacred – perhaps note a few special days of your own: anniversaries, seasonal days…

You may want to honour them with some time in meditation.

Use your journal to make note of times you find particularly challenging – do you struggle to fall asleep? Do you find the change of seasons hard? Perhaps note times where a meditation practice may help you find balance or cultivate empowerment.

You can start and end each day with a simple gratitude practice of listing (on paper or in your mind) what you are grateful for or looking forward to. This can be part of a meditation, or simply a wonderful task to do while you are waiting at the bus stop or for the kettle to boil!

Find little moments of stillness and mindfulness through the day. Slow down for longer whenever you can.

It is my hope that you will return to these meditations again and again, you will find that your meditative journey may well change with each and every listening.

I wish you love and blessings, wherever you are now and wherever you travel on your journey.

CYCLES
DAYS AND SEASONS

The cycles of the year can offer a wonderful guide for our energy work — whether that be yoga, spell craft or meditation. The wheel shifts from day to night, season into season, the cycle of the year will always turn. In observing and honouring the seasons we may well learn how to take care of ourselves and our energy: living in harmony with the seasons and days can bring greater health and peace.

Spring

Spring Seeds

It's spring! The sun has returned, and the days are growing longer. It's time to begin to unravel and unfurl. Just like seeds in the springtime, we can take in that which nourishes us so we can expand and grow.

This is a short and sweet spring meditation to start your process of growth.

Allow yourself to settle into the safe place you have chosen for your meditation. Make sure you're warm and comfortable. Begin to relax into this place, and gently close your eyes. Taking a nice deep breath in. And exhaling. Easeful inhales. Easeful exhales.

As you begin to slow the breath and bring your attention inwards, let a feeling of calm and well-being spread throughout your body. Know that you are safe and allow yourself this time to settle and surrender into the earth.

Pause

And now, as you rest in this place, in line with the spring season, I want you to envisage that you are a seed: small and shining, full of possibility.

As your seed self, you have been planted into the earth, nestled in the soft ground. And as this seed, you have been sleeping, resting through the dark winter. And you have been dreaming about the plant that you will become; it might be a beautiful flower or healing herb, a fruit bush of bright berries or a great tall tree of the forest. Allow yourself to visualise this plant, whatever it may be.

Pause

The time has now come for a new cycle to begin, the season of spring beckons with open arms and rosy fingers. It is time for you to start a journey to awakening. You may visualise the light of the spring sun and begin to feel gentle energy and warmth moving through you. You may begin to gently reach out, breaking out of your shell.

Visualise sending roots down deep into the earth so that you can draw in what nourishes you. These roots travel downwards into grounding, giving you strong foundations, drawing in nourishment and feeding your journey of growth. Now you also begin expanding upwards. Unfurling, stem and stalk reaching upward to the sun. Your first green shoots, your first green leaves appear. The growing light and warmth of the spring sunshine gently draws you, guiding you to reach skywards.

You and the elements of sky and earth, above and below, entwine in harmonious rhythm of drawing in and expanding out. Drawing in what nourishes you. Unfurling, unravelling, growing more leaves, deeper roots, rising in growth. Drawing in and reaching out, breathing in and breathing out. Taking up space, feeling into expansion. As you continue to grow and rise, you are in a process of becoming: becoming who you are or who you wish to be.

Let yourself stay with this feeling of growth. With every breath; you are taking in what you need; expanding and growing. You can stay here as long as you wish. This process does not need to be quick: we grow and bloom and blossom in our own time as our own beautiful spring shoots. Just when you feel ready, you may open your eyes.

Journaling Ideas

You may spend a few quiet minutes here or take time to journal about what nourishes you, what it means to you to draw on deep **roots, and** what growth means to you. Or even **draw** a picture of the plant you wish to become.

Riding White Horses

Our meditation today will take us on a journey with the Celtic/Roman goddess, Epona.* She is a goddess that is often depicted as either a beautiful white horse or riding one. I am particularly fond of this goddess, not least because on the hills near my West Country home, there are several white chalk horses carved into hillsides. And whispers of goddess Epona were left by the Romans in sacred spaces in Aquae Sulis (now my beloved city of Bath, UK).

In Epona's connection to horses, she represents freedom, travel, transformation, the ability and power to pass into different realms and over thresholds. In our meditation today, I will take some time to guide you through a few images. But also give you a little time of quiet to have the freedom to allow your own mind to wander and roam like a wild horse.

Find the place you wish to rest. Make sure that you are warm and comfortable. As we begin to settle through the body, we find this place of safety, calm within a restful place.

We let go of tension and tightness. And then let go of anything we might be holding onto. So that the body settles and the breath is peaceful.

Pause

We bring the mind to the freedom of springtime. I often think of Epona during the springtime and at spring equinox

---

*   Pronounced *eh-POH-na*

where we are gifted a sense of space, light and freedom to venture out as the days grow longer.

In your mind's eye, envisage yourself riding on a white horse. A calm and gentle companion. Walking gently through a field in the springtime sun. New green shoots with golden spring flowers dance around you. A few perhaps getting crumpled under your horse's hooves, sending up that beautiful springtime scent of earth and sunshine and flowers.

From your perch on top of your horse, you can see a little further around you. Perhaps you see past the fields and to trees and hills and mountains beyond. There is a feeling of lightness and joy and connection with this horse. You may have a sense of the goddess Epona watching over you on this gentle journey. Perhaps you envisage her riding beside you on her own horse. Or maybe she is the horse. Her energy, her image, her archetype can be embodied in any way that feels right for you.

The light and the warmth of the day seem to fill both you and your horse with a sense of lightness and freedom. The pace quickens a little and you begin to gently trot. Maybe you even move into a canter or gallop. Whichever you choose, you enjoy the smooth, powerful movement. You run through fields and meadows. Perhaps you are weaving through trees now, or even on a sandy beach riding in sunshine and sparkling surf.

You take a journey through the sunlight, through nature. Sights and sounds and smells of the natural world weave around you. You find yourself smiling, maybe even laughing, with this sense of total exhilaration.

Your horse begins to gently slow. From gallop to canter to trot, and then a gentle walk once more. You see that you have journeyed to a special place. Wherever you have travelled through, you now find yourself on a green hill with a beautiful ancient tree at its peak. Once you reach the shade of the tree, you dismount your horse and both take a little time to rest. You drink some water and breathe in the scents and sights of this special place, so peaceful and calm. Your horse companion gently nuzzles you with their nose, like soft velvet. You thank them for this journey today, and being your companion here. An understanding passes between you.

And now the beautiful white horse turns to go. It is time for them to take their own journey. They leave you and you see them walking back down the hill. Maybe they are joined by other horses. You are filled with a sense of gratitude that you were able to enjoy this special moment with this fleeting beauty. This wild creature. This embodiment of strength and power and grace. These beautiful qualities are within you as well, and perhaps a little time with the white horses and goddess Epona in the springtime sun is just what you needed to remind you.

Pause

And with this little pause from your journey, you take time to rest and restore and know that you have the power – to take those next steps of your path, whatever they may be. The power of the white horse and of the great goddess are with you always.

And so, my dear ones, there is no rush. In your own time, take some deep breaths and a stretch or a movement of the body as you begin to bring yourself back to the room and back to your day. When you feel ready, you can gently open the eyes. I hope that you enjoyed this little journey with the goddess and the white horses.

Summer

A Swim in Summer

Take a rejuvenating dip in sparkling waters on a summer's day. A short and bright meditation to find a little peace on a sunny day, and an invitation to feel refreshed, revived and reinvigorated. If you are able to be outside then do this meditation outdoors, it might be resting on the grass or seated on the earth. If you're inside, it may be on your favourite chair or soft place.

Find a comfortable seated position. Close your eyes and take five conscious deep breaths. Inhaling deeply through your nose. And exhaling slowly through your mouth. With each breath, notice your body begin to relax.

Pause

Now, we'll envisage that we are sitting outside under rays of bright sunshine. If you are in fact seated outside, then all the better. The sun shines overhead and you feel its warmth brighten your body. One part at a time. Starting with your toes. They feel warm and comforted. The light moves up over your legs, hips, tummy, chest and heart. Light and warmth. The sun shines over your shoulders, arms, neck, and face. And finally, the very top of your head. Notice the sun's warmth covering every single part of you. From the tips of your toes to the top of your head. Notice how it feels, to bask in the warmth of the sun. Take your time to enjoy, to savour this warmth.

Now, visualise in front of you a body of water. It could be a lake, still and sparkling. It could be an ocean, a river or a beautiful turquoise swimming pool. Take your time as you gently rise in your mind's eye from your seated place. Take a deep inhale and dive into the water. Notice how the water feels on your face and skin. Feel the sensation of the cooling water as you dive in. Diving deeper and deeper. Feel the sensations of diving deep into the water. Cool, calm and quiet. You start to rise and come up to the surface. You take a nice deep breath of air before diving back in under the water. Descending once more into the depths, into the quiet. And once more you ascend to the surface. Take a nice deep breath. Here on the sparkling surface of this water you feel both the refreshing water and the warming sun. The breeze kissing your cheeks and the light sparkling and bouncing off the water around you. Take your time to feel these sensations. To feel the warmth and the cool. To experience the light and the water around you.

And as the moment comes to leave the water, take your time to find your way easefully back to dry land. Notice your transition of slowly rising from the water. The air feels cool on your skin. The soft earth beneath your feet. The sun's rays warm and dry your face, your arms, your entire body. Feel the sun's warmth dry and soothe you from head to toe. And when you feel dry and warm, you once more return in your mind's eye to your peaceful seat in the sunshine. Bringing awareness back to your breath. Slow inhales and exhales. Take one more deep breath in through the nose. And out through the mouth.

Gently open your eyes. And lean into the calmness of the mind and the body as you return to your summer's day. May your day be blissful, calm and filled with joy.

Mindfulness

Mindfulness is a state of awareness of the present moment, greeting and accepting feelings, thoughts, and bodily sensations as they arise. Minds wander, and we can lose touch with our bodies, engrossed in thoughts, worries or regrets.

Mindfulness is the cultivation of the ability to be fully present; to bring our attention back to where we are, bringing the mind to fully attend to what's happening. Meditation, as I have already mentioned, is also a practice of finding focus. A more modern word for this is mindfulness. Mindfulness and meditation are two names for what is, in essence, the same practice. Any activity can be done with mindfulness: walking, running, knitting, gardening…which can in turn help us inhabit the present moment and improve focus.

Simple Sunlight Mindfulness

Almost all of the meditations in this book are guided visual-isations as they lend themselves best to these guided scripts. However, during the summer, when we can grow busy with plans, adventures, holidays, barbecues and parties it can be lovely simply to spend a little time basking in the sun (or in the shade of a tree) and enjoying the moment. Absorbing the warmth of summer like the sunflowers, like the trees, like the leaves. We, like many things in nature, benefit from absorbing the light of this great star.

So here all I suggest that you do, in a simple mindfulness practice is to find your place, close your eyes or gaze skywards (with suitable sunglasses), perhaps set a timer if you wish for five minutes.

Let the light shine upon you, feel the sensation of the warmth upon your skin, see the colours around you if your eyes are open, or the glow behind your eyelids. Smell the scent of green grass, of flowers, of dry earth. Hear the sound of birds, children playing, of laughter. Use all your senses to enjoy this simple moment on a sunny day.

Pause

When you're ready take a stretch and move on with your day. And maybe throughout the summer take these little pauses to revel in the light of the season.

The Green Witch's Garden

For many centuries, to be called a witch was not a positive thing. However, these wise women, these healing men, had knowledge, wisdom and amazing skills that I want to bring forward into our work here in meditation. So, we are drawing out the positives. I don't want to forget the history, but I do want to celebrate this freedom we have now have to draw on the skills and the wisdom of the witches. Today we'll walk within the realms of the Green Witch, the witch of healing, growth and seasons. In a beautiful remembering we can rediscover whispers of the past: a history of witches, fairies, and magic, within folk-lore and folk names of plants. The echoes of magic are still here.

So, let's journey to find a little of that magic and memory. Take your time, make yourself warm and comfortable. The more you can allow the body to relax, the easier the mind can find it to roam in our visualisations. So, as you settle into your place, let the body fall into softness.

Pause

From this place of calm we envisage in our mind's eye that beautiful sensation of bare feet on warm sunlit grass. Lush green grass beneath your feet. Between your toes. A solidity beneath you. Supporting you. A sense that in a busy world, amongst busy thoughts, here is our truest teacher, our most steadfast guide: the earth beneath our feet. As you lift your gaze from this beautiful grass and earth beneath you, you see now that you are in a beautiful garden. The sun is shining in a clear summer sky above you. You feel welcomed into this space. Warmed by its gentle magic.

And it may be that there is an image in your mind, of a gentle person. A custodian of this garden welcoming you in. Or maybe it is the garden itself, the swaying grasses in the sunlight that seem to wave you welcome. You have a deep sense that this beautiful place is one of magic. There is magic and memory within this garden. Allow yourself to see the blossoms and smell their scent. See them gently dance and sway in the warm breeze, their roots running deep into the earth.

The name Green Witch is a modern one. A beautiful name to capture the essence of the wise one who tends plants and herbs and sees the magical potential of healing within them.

My ancestors called the bluebells and the foxgloves, fairy bells and witches thimbles, a reminder that there is magic in the garden. Plants of vines and creepers might be used to catch and entangle negative energy. In the plant we call ragweed, stories are held of a method of flight for fairies and witches. But the flight that is really held within the leaves, perhaps, is one of lifting the mood, of lightening and brightening our senses. Within each little story from folklore there is a truth. The comfort of these messages, ideas, these ancestral memories of mine. But now. Let's look at yours.

Perhaps you first see plants and herbs that you recognise. They might be favourites of yours: beautiful blooms and blossoms you love. You might see healing herbs used in teas and tinctures. Memories of these plants' properties may run back so far you cannot remember where this knowledge came from. You simply know.

Here, in the light of the sun, in the sway of the plants, you may see a beloved family member who enjoyed growing flowers in their garden. Maybe a grandmother who knew just what to do with those seasonal vegetables to create a delicious feast. Or a caregiver who knew how to brew a cup of herbal tea to soothe and comfort. Maybe a teacher or a guide that showed you the beauty to be found within the garden and the natural world. Maybe the person you see is yourself. Maybe you see yourself in child form. Enjoying dancing through the grass. Running your hands through tall stems.

With excitement and intrigue your inner child sees the magic of the garden, without the need for rules. You know there is magic here. You are born with that knowledge. Take some peaceful moments in this beautiful place. Surrounded by those who have walked this path, ones we may call the Green Witch. Or we may know them as loved ones who are gardeners, growers, nurturers and nourishers. There is a little sparkle of magic within them all because there's a sparkle of that knowledge, the healing power of the natural world.

Pause

And so, as you prepare yourself to leave this blissful summer garden, just for now, feel free to give yourself time to hug or wish a fond farewell to anyone you have met in the garden. Perhaps gentle beams of sunlight shine down upon them, and they gently glow and disappear, to be held within your heart, mind and memory.

Take as long as you need to return from the journey.

Journaling Ideas

If you wish to do so, take a few notes of those who you met in the garden and what they taught you, in their own way, about the plants and the flowers. Whether it was lessons or a story or simply reflected in their love of the land. This is an opportunity to connect more deeply to that beautiful memory and the memories of those who have taught us, in our own way.

Autumn

The Story of Persephone and Demeter

With this short story and guided meditation, we journey with ancient Greek goddesses Persephone, Demeter, and Hecate* to embrace change in this autumnal season.

This story of Persephone and her mother, the goddess Demeter, can be a challenging one, as Persephone's fate is decided for her. But I do believe there is hope to be found and a certain inspiration.

Let's begin with a short story, a tale of myth and magic and the Underworld. After the story, we will journey into a little guided meditation, so feel free to take your time now to get comfortable. Get yourself a drink or wrap yourself in a blanket, lie down and close your eyes.

Pause

---

*   Pronounced *Per-SEF-o-nee, Di-MEE-ter* and *HEK-uh-tee* (this is the most common UK and US pronunciation, although the more correct Greek pronunciation is *He-KAH-tay*.)

Persephone and the Pomegranate Seeds

Persephone is picking flowers from a meadow when Hades,[†] god of the Underworld, rising from the Earth, carries her away to be his bride in the Underworld. The goddess Hecate hears the cries of poor Persephone and goes to tell her mother, goddess of the harvest, Demeter. Together they search for her. Hecate guides Demeter through the dark nights with flaming torches to light her way through the many crossroads and paths of the Underworld and its eternal night. But to no avail.

Demeter is so grief-stricken that she casts the Earth into barrenness. No crops can grow as she mourns. The people of the land are starving. So Persephone's father, the god Zeus,[‡] is forced to order Hades to release her from the Underworld. Hades agrees to let her go, but not before first entreating her to eat some pomegranate seeds, which she does. Having consumed food of the Underworld she becomes part of this realm and must then spend half a year here, every year. She is now Queen of the Underworld and goddess of death, though against her will, she has claimed a powerful role. However, when Persephone returns to her

---

†   Pronounced *HAY-deez*

‡   Pronounced *Zjus* (UK) *zus* (US)

mother each spring, Demeter ensures that the season flourishes. The pomegranate trees blossom and the Earth again produces flowers, fruit and grain. But when autumn falls, Persephone must return to the Underworld. Hecate, returning once more, becomes her companion on her yearly journeys and helps lead her through the realms. And the Earth falls into dormancy of the dark winter months as Demeter grieves the loss of her daughter each year.

This is the story of Persephone and Demeter. Of the many themes present within this tale of classical mythology, there's the theme of change: the changes of the seasons, the changes of life and changes that are not necessarily our choice, but ones that we may claim, should we wish.

Meditation

So with this simple idea of coming to a place of darkness, I invite you to find your restful place if you are not there already. Close your eyes. Within our mind's eye, we will make our own journey down into the Earth. We might come across a tunnel or a set of stairs that lead us downwards. And though we are journeying down into a darker place there is still light in the form of candles or lanterns, perhaps. Perhaps you are holding a torch to light your way. This place is quiet and peaceful, and as you journey down, down, into the Underworld, you sense the noise and the busyness of the world outside gently softening as you move to a place that is a little quieter, a little more still.

As we come to the end of our pathway, those steps, or the

corridor that leads us downwards, we find a room. This is our own special place beneath the Earth, our own place of quiet and calm: a sanctuary. As you enter, you may see a beautiful, sacred space, a temple with candles and altar. Or perhaps a very cosy room strewn with velvet cushions and blankets and a gently crackling hearth fire. Maybe the space is a beautiful old library: the walls covered in books and gilded colours. So quiet and peaceful. Take your time to visualise your space.

And in your space, you may feel a sensation of being gently watched over, after all the goddess Persephone dwells here, within the Underworld. In this, the season of autumn and winter, she watches over you with a kind heart. For she knows the sorrows and hurts of so many things that are beyond our control. But in this space of quiet and dark, know that you may rest from it all. This is a place where you may find some peace.

Pause of a minute or more

When the time comes to leave the sacred space, know that you can return here any time you wish. For this place will be here whenever you need to come back to quiet and darkness. Persephone smiles. A brightness appears behind you. The goddess Hecate has brought her bright torches to help guide you back towards the Earth's surface and back, perhaps to a little more noise and busyness, the hustle and bustle of the day. We leave Persephone in the quiet place, wishing her farewell for now. Hecate smiles as she guides you along the pathway. Back to the day.

Demeter is here to meet you. She smiles and embraces you and welcomes you back to the world above. Perhaps you hear birds calling or hear trees swaying in the breeze. Perhaps some trees still hold gold, red and brown leaves that are ready to dance in the breeze as autumn progresses. Demeter is here and she is waiting. She is waiting for the return of her daughter and knows that that day will come. When the season will once more burst into light and joy and brightness. For now we rest. We wait. We find value in this time of dormancy. And when we need it, we know that there is guidance and love, that we are being watched over by the guardian goddesses: Persephone, Demeter and Hecate.

Pause

Take your time to stretch as we begin to ever so gently bring our awareness back to the day and back to the room. Take a nice deep breath. Wriggle the body. Whatever you like. We'll just rise up to an easy seat. Take a nice stretch towards the sky.

I welcome you back! In the season of autumn, we have a little more darkness, but also a chance to let go and find a little peace in the stillness. I wish you well on your onward journey as we move through the seasons.

The Bonfire Circle

This season is one of bonfires: Samhain,[*] Bonfire Night,[†] and other age-old celebrations where we gather and bring a lightness into the season that rolls into darkness. In this simple meditation we will use that beautiful image of both the bonfire and of gathering around the fire in circle, an ancient, sacred, simple but powerful practice of our earliest ancestors for warmth, nourishment, connection and comfort.

We will settle, relax and close the eyes.

I want you to envisage a place in nature, a place where you feel safe, a place you enjoy, or that is connected to positive memories. It might be a beach, a field, a garden, a park… Take your time to create this place in your mind's eye, take in the sights, and smells, and sounds.

Pause

In this place you'll see a beautiful dancing bonfire with gold, yellow, orange plumes of light, smoke rising and that familiar scent in the air. As you approach this bonfire you see that there is a circle of people around the flames. This circle is your circle. Many faces turn and smile as you approach, and they take a step back to create space for you to join them. You see now, in the dancing fire light, a circle of people who mean something

---

[*]   Pronounced *SOW-in*. This is the Irish and Scots Gaelic term for the festival we call Halloween in English.

[†]   A British festival celebrated with bonfires and fireworks on 5th November.

to you – they might be loved ones, family or friends, they might be people who inspire you, people of whom you have fond memories, people you have worked with… There may even be spirits, animals or deities, anyone and anything that has helped you and that brings sparkle to your life can be in this circle. Take your time to see them, feel them.

Here in this circle we stand. We might share smiles and laughter, tell stories or simply enjoy being quiet together watching the flames. A warmth spreads within your heart. It is both from these flames, and maybe more so, from this circle of souls around you.

Pause

When the time comes to leave this beautiful circle, we all take a step back to create an opening – the circle is open, but never broken. The love, the inspiration, the contribution of these souls, these people, these energies have brought to your life can never be taken away from you. This circle exists within you always, forming a halo around your heart. Take a moment here if you wish to hug and bid fond farewell to these beings in your circle.

And, with your heart still glowing from the light of these souls and this beautiful energy of coming together in circle held within you, we'll take some nice deep breaths, perhaps stretch the body, wiggle the toes… When you are ready, come back to the room and open your eyes. Welcome back!

Winter

Mother Night

The Yule festivals were very important to the northern Euro-pean cultures, recipients of some of the darkest and harshest winters. For the Anglo-Saxons, the time of midwinter and the longest night, winter solstice, was called Modranicht* – Mother Night. You may wish to use this simple meditation to prepare for ritual or find a peaceful moment for journaling or spellwork.

Welcome to midwinter, the longest night and winter solstice. To my Anglo-Saxon ancestors, this is *Modranicht,* the Mother Night. A chance, perhaps, to connect to female ancestors and acknowledge the primal darkness that will bear the new year. Here in this simple and quiet meditation, I offer a chance to allow yourself to be wrapped in the arms of Mother Night. To find a little quiet, a little sanctuary in this, the darkest and longest of nights. Comforted in the knowledge that each day after this one will grow a little lighter.

Here, on Mother Night, we are all children of the dark, the

---

* Pronounced *MO-dra-nickht*

cold, the quiet. Perhaps it is a chance to take a sacred pause. I invite you to close your eyes and find a place that is warm and calm within, a few minutes to find your own place of quiet. Allowing your body to settle heavy and restful upon the Earth. Calm of breath and calm of mind. As we take some peaceful minutes in the dark.

Take a few quiet minutes

Let us take a deep breath, gently move the body. If you are peaceful where you are, then by all means stay in restfulness. If you would like to gently rise to seated, we'll take a moment just to sit within this space. Quiet and calm.

I wish you a warm, safe and merry midwinter and Mother Night.

Journaling Ideas

If you are using this meditation as the beginning of a ritual or to prompt your journal practice, feel free to take as long as you need. Feel the energy of the Mother Night within you, write any words or intentions, or light a candle or any ritual you wish, for the coming days.

Midwinter Magic: Meeting the Cailleach

Enjoy a journey with the Cailleach,* the Celtic crone goddess and queen of winter. During the darkest months, she sweeps her cloak of winter white over the land, freezing the ground. The personification of the elemental power of nature, the Cailleach is the creatrix of the land: she carves rocks and mountains to serve as her stepping-stones.

For today's meditation, I'd love to connect you to the Celtic goddess of winter: the Cailleach. Her name literally means old one or crone, and she is represented as a beautiful old woman with white hair. She's the embodiment of winter and the cold elements of the land.

To prepare yourself to journey with the Cailleach today, take your time and settle into a cosy place, because where we're going is very cold. Wrap yourself up warm. Gently close the eyes and we'll begin to let the breath be calm. Let the noise of the world fall into soft focus. And here in our mind's eye, we journey and find ourselves.

Pause

We find ourselves amongst the snow of Scotland: the highlands, the great mountains are looming around us. They say that the Cailleach dropped these rocks so that she could leap and move through the land. These mountains are her stepping-stones.

---

*   Cailleach can be pronounced *KAY-lackh* or *KAI-lyackh* in Irish and Scots Gaelic dependant on regional accent.

As soon as you think of this goddess of winter, with her white mantle of snow that sweeps over the lands, it is as though you have called her. Because no sooner have you thought of her, she arrives by your side almost as light as the snow around her. She is so light and bright, and she moves as quietly as the falling snow. This beautiful old woman holds out a small hand. And you take hold of it. It is warm and soft.

She wants to guide you on a journey. And even though she does not speak to you, she smiles, and you feel that she is friendly, warm and welcoming in this land of snow that she calls her home.

She moves so smoothly over the snow. At first you think she must have very steady feet...but in fact she is not walking, but flying. And before you know it, your feet have also left the ground as you sweep up the mountainsides. You see the white of the snow sweep beneath you and you rise and rise towards a clear blue sky. You rise towards mountains topped with snow, white and bright in the sun. Sweeping through the mountains, you spot the great white wings of owls and little ptarmigans[*] also flying up the slopes, as though they are playing a game and joining you on your flight. You feel as light as snow, as light as a feather.

The goddess takes you to the very peak of the snowy mountains, sheltered from the wind, in a place that feels soundless. You come back down to the ground here, at the peak of the mountain, in a sheltered spot. Your feet rest upon the snow. The winter goddess lays out soft white blankets upon

---

[*]   Pronounced *TAR-mi-gan*. A bird like a partridge or grouse which develops white plumage during the winter months.

the snow and wraps you in them. Then, with a skill of many years' practice, she lays out a fire and lights it, creating a flickering warmth that casts shadows upon the snow. You feel warm and comfortable, able to take in the beautiful, sparkling sights around you. All is quiet, and you feel at peace.

This crone goddess is a wild woman, connected to all the wilderness and nature of the Earth. And as you sit in the comfort of the elements of the fire and the snow, she encourages you to connect to your own inner wild soul, the untamed and passionate being within you. This idea of the divine feminine and the feminine wild is within all of us, whatever our gender. The feminine is intuitive and powerful if we allow it, in tune with the ebbs and flows of energies of the world and the power of the elements. This energy helps us connect with our own inner goddess, our inner wise one. The wise, crone goddess Cailleach is so ancient. She knows the ways of the world and how to connect with all the elements. It may be that as you look upon this fire now in the special place of snow and calm, the goddess has a word of wisdom or two for you. She may speak it aloud or guide you to a knowing or an intuition of your own.

You may hear it now within this meditation, or it may come to you in the next few days. There is no right or wrong. So do not worry about how this message may arrive. And do not worry if nothing comes to you right now. Just allow yourself to be in this peaceful place of snow and flickering flames. This beautiful place of the elements and the power of nature.

Pause

Soon enough, the time has come to leave this special place.

The goddess holds out a warm hand, and you shrug off your blankets. Once again, you take an exhilarating flight along the slopes of the mountains that the goddess herself uses as her stepping-stones through the land. Like birds in flight, you sweep down the side of the mountain to once more bring your feet onto solid ground. Take a moment to gaze up at the beauty around you.

The Cailleach smiles. When you are set down upon the earth and ready to take your next steps, she sweeps up her white mantle and once again, like a soundless owl, she has gone.

Here amongst the snow, you have found the beautiful and strong power of the winter, of the cold and of the goddess. May you carry it with you. May it keep you warm in your next steps on your journey, underneath the cold winter skies.

Morning

Start your day with a little positivity. These practices may help you to let go of troubles, worries and those inner voices that can return again and again. Sometimes we are able to let go, some days we find it more of a challenge. And that's okay. This isn't about finding perfection. As we practice our meditation we grow stronger and more able to let go, so the process becomes easier!

All of these morning meditations are perfect to do seated, even perhaps with a warm drink.

Wild Dawn

This is a journey to embrace the hope and possibility of the dawn. If you are able to rise before the dawn and take a walk out into the natural world, that is beautiful, but perhaps we are just somewhere safe and warm inside. Perhaps it is early morning. Maybe it's any time of day, and we take this pause just to close the eyes and take a moment to settle and relax.

We find ourselves in our mind's eye in a beautiful place in nature. Somewhere that we have a beautiful view of the horizon and the sky…perhaps a mountain top or a hill or a forest clearing. The sun has not yet kissed the horizon on its rising journey, but there is that gentle light in the sky, we see dusky colours. We know that the light is coming.

With the coming light, there is a sense of hope. Possibility.

And it's not just us that feel this. As the dawn approaches, we hear from the trees around us, the dawn chorus, as birds rise and sing to their kin. A celebration of song, a connection, a declaration, this beautiful song to announce that they have made it through the night and a new day is coming.

The first flashes of the sun begin to rise over the horizon. The sky lights up in shades of pink and orange and red. It is aglow with light. And now the singing birds begin to rise in flight. You see these beautiful birds flying up into the sky around you. They rise as the sun rises.

As the sun rises higher, the light grows. It is skimming past the horizon now. You feel the sense of lift within you is growing like this rising of the sun and these birds in flight.

Before you is a day that you can make your own. You can fill this day with the things that bring you joy, that help lift you and others up. Take your time to visualise now in the full light of the morning sun, your day ahead, your week ahead. How can you embrace this gift of time, this gift of a new day?

There may be challenges and adventures ahead. Celebrate the unknown, the wildness, the potential of a new dawn and embrace this bright new day.

Journaling Ideas

So, wild travellers, this is your opportunity now, if you wish, to make your list or set your intentions. They can be as simple and complex as you like. You might like to note down a list of all that you wish to achieve today or simply hold it in your mind. How might you nurture your connections to the natural world today? How might you aid your rising and singing like the birds? Or you may simply wish to move into your day with a sense of calm and an intention to be mindful. Take as long as you need to set your intentions, your goals, your dreams, whatever they may be.

Letting Go

Good morning, friends. Welcome to this morning meditation for letting go. As you settle in a comfortable seated position, we'll take some nice deep breaths, filling the lungs. Inhale, exhale, inhale, exhale. Continue with these easeful breaths as we take our first moments in our brand-new morning.

Pause

We will reflect on letting go. Letting go of the whispers from yesterday. Letting go of worries and concerns. The inner voices of criticism and self-doubt. Each and every time you exhale or breathe out, let everything that you can release fall away from your body.

Each new day will bring challenges and new whispers of

worry, doubt and criticism. But each day we can return to our meditation. Each day we can start our morning by letting go. Cleaning the slate.

Some days it will feel easy to let go, to shrug off these weights we carry upon our shoulders. Some days it will be hard. But know this, dearest: each and every time we practice letting go, we grow stronger. We come back each and every day returning to our meditation and letting go of anything we do not need to carry into this brand new day.

As you continue your restful breaths this morning, feel free to acknowledge anything that arises for you, whether it be fear or nervousness, doubt, anger or frustration. Allow yourself to reflect on what the day ahead may hold, whilst letting go of anything that lingers from yesterday which does not serve you.

Life can be tough, dear one, but you are tougher. You are stronger. You can overcome and let go, carry with you only what you need to support you and bring you strength and comfort in this new day. Allow yourself to let go, or set the intention to let go. Celebrate that which you are able to let go of. But do not worry if you are not able to today. Sometimes we may hold on to something that is simple to let go of: an argument we've had or a cross word. We can let that go. If the journey is longer, such as a period of grieving or healing, give yourself time. There is no judgement here in our meditation space. Simply intention. To let go. Each and every time we need to, each and every time the chance is available to us.

So let us move into this new day with a lightness, brightness and hope.

Pause

Welcome to a brand new day, my darlings. As you stretch and move and rise from your meditation, step forward with strength, with power and make your way into your journey and into your day, with love and acceptance.

Morning Affirmations

Get comfortable in a seated position and repeat quietly in your mind, "Today is a new day." Breathe slowly and deeply. Imagine a vibrant yellow light flowing into your body with every breath you take. This bright, beautiful light is charged with a positive energy. So, with every breath you take, your body draws in a little more light, a little more energy, becoming naturally energised. This positive energy spreads throughout your whole body, recharging every cell, every part of you.

You feel your body and your own energy charged with this positive, vibrant light. Embrace this feeling. You feel joyful and you look forward to your day. Looking forward to the adventures that lie ahead. Give yourself permission to feel wonderful. And to feel wonderful about yourself. You can say these following words in your mind or out loud:

I breathe.

I feel.

I am energised.[*]

---

[*] Affirmations are very personal to your own journey, so you may well add "I am working towards feeling…" before any of these words if that feels more appropriate for you. Feel free to leave out some statements, or add your own.

Quietly aware, in the back of your mind, that with every breath you take, your body and energy will continue to recharge, so keep those breaths long and deep. And now, I want you to gently smile to yourself. Pay attention to how that simple little smile improves your mood. And try and keep that gentle smile on your face while you repeat the following, either out loud or in your mind:

I am taking steps towards a life I love.

I am grateful for my life.

I send love to the person I am.

I am building confidence.

I am loved.

I am happy.

I am safe and I feel safe.

Today, everything can be fun and easy.

Today, wonderful things can happen.

I am allowing myself to enjoy this day.

Today is a new day.

Pause

So, it's time, my darlings, to begin your wonderful new day. Perhaps we give the fingers and toes a little wiggle, a little movement, maybe stretch or roll the shoulders. And when you open your eyes, you will be wide awake, feeling energised and ready for a great day. Open your eyes and enjoy your day!

Mantra

A mantra is a word or short phrase that is repeated to support meditation practice. Mantras can help harness the power of words and language to focus the mind. Simple mantras can be added to meditation, ritual or spell work, and can be a powerful tool to help the conscious mind to relax, quietening internal dialogue. One of the best-known mantras in yoga practice is *Om*. In Hindu mythology this was the first sound of the universe, so it represents the birth, death and re-birth process. *Om* is a powerful mantra, but in your own language there are many that many mean something more to you: Love, Breath, Rest…can all be very special too.

Evening and Night

An Evening Woodland Walk

This is a simple guided journey to help you let go of your work-day and ease into your evening at home – warm, content and relaxed. As we take a walk in the golden evening light, we will use natural imagery to help find peace.

Welcome to this meditation for the end of the day. Take your time to find a comfortable place, seated or lying down, make sure that you have any support that you need to feel restful. Here, my darlings, in this place, we celebrate the end of our day. Perhaps the end of a day that has been busy and noisy. Here we seek to cross over a threshold and leave behind the stresses of the day, easing gently into the evening as we settle in our restful space. Perhaps closing the eyes or letting the gaze be soft as we allow the body to soften and relax.

Pause

We'll take a gentle journey in our mind's eye. To start this journey, we first discard the clothing of our day, whether that be a business suit or another kind of uniform, or simply the clothes that we have worn during the day – we cast them aside. Perhaps we now dress ourselves in our favourite clothes, our softest and warmest clothes, or maybe our most treasured. Maybe we pull on our favourite ball gown with our cosiest slippers. Or our pajamas and our favourite hat. And as you dress yourself for your evening, maybe you wrap around yourself a beautiful cloak coloured like the evening: with navy and blues, and indigos and deep, dark black. Maybe there are sparkles upon this cape to reflect the stars that may soon begin to appear in the night sky. Though you are looking forward to settling in your warm and comfortable home, before that, we are going to take an easeful journey.

Wrapped beautifully in our evening wear, we leave our front door and find dusk hovering in the sky. The sun is setting. This is the golden hour, when the sun casts golden light through trees and over fields. Take a gentle walk through nature to say goodbye to the day. Perhaps you walk on soft green grass or a woodland path. All nature has been busy through the day. In the beautiful golden light of the evening, you see birds flying home to roost, small animals gathering up leaves and seeds to carry home to their burrows. Just like you, they are collecting what they need to draw home. So, as you enjoy the last light of the day, as you watch the birds and the animals going to their homes, let those final rays of sunlight bring light that washes away your day, whatever adventures, whatever joys, whatever highs, whatever lows, we gather them in, file them away or let them go now.

Walking through nature, we remind ourselves of the cycle of all things.

The day has passed and soon the night will arrive. And we must give ourselves a chance to rest so that when the sun rises tomorrow we feel able, just like the birds, to take flight once more and to journey through our day.

Pause

As the golden hour comes to an end, night is almost upon us. Perhaps the first few stars are visible in the sky. It is time to draw homewards, and as you find yourself once more looking at your home, in whatever form it takes in your meditation, we'll take a moment before we step inwards, to savour with gratitude a warm home, the shelter, the light that awaits us within.

And as you step through your front door, you feel ready. Able to let go of your day. To find your path in the cycle of day and night as you move into this restful evening.

You can cast aside your cape, peel away the layers to reveal whatever comfortable clothing you now wish to wear. In this restful space of the evening, as the light dims outside, maybe you light candles, lamps or a fire. As the sky darkens, your home comes to life with warmth and light: a shelter, a refuge, and a sanctuary. You are home. May you move through your evening with restful gratitude and a sense of warmth and peace.

Take as long as you need to breathe and relax, find a moment of peace that you can carry into your evening and night. I wish you a good evening and good night.

The Warrior Rests

We are all of us warriors, doing battle each day to work challenging jobs, to speak our truth. Perhaps we battle with chronic illness or injury, carry daily worries, or hustle to get through the day and earn money for our family. The warrior goddess Diana will help guide us through a practice of resting, setting down our armour, and washing away the day.

Welcome to this meditation inspired by the Roman goddess Diana. Diana is the goddess of the hunt, of wild animals, woodland, and the moon. She is a powerful huntress and a beautiful goddess who will guide us in meditation this evening as we learn to embody her.

Take a little time here to allow yourself to relax. Create a soft and warm space in which you can sit or lie down comfortably. Gently close your eyes. Allow your breath to be your focus. Allow the rise and fall of the breath to gently guide you into a place of calm and peace. With each inhale draw in a little peace, a little calm, a little restfulness. And with each

exhale a letting go. Let go of the busy thoughts of your day, let go of the stresses and worries that you carry with you, even if it is just for the next few minutes.

Pause

From this place of restfulness and ease, imagine yourself walking slowly through a lush green forest. Dusk is falling and the sky above you is darkening with beautiful shades of colour. Tall trees rise to the sky around you. You walk slowly and calmly, perhaps with a little weariness from your day, through the forest.

You carry with you a great silver bow in your arms. You are clad in shining armour. As you continue to walk through the forest, you come to a clearing. Dusk has now passed, and a great moon has risen in the sky. It casts a beautiful silvery light on this clearing. You notice that running through this space is a babbling brook, a gentle stream of sparkling splashes. Making your way to the water you see for the first time your reflection. Clad in beautiful, shining armour, carrying your silver bow. You are strong and you are powerful. Even if perhaps, you don't feel that way right now. You have fought great battles today. Do not forget that.

Whether those battles were rising early with the alarm clock, heading for a long day of work to earn money to put food on the table. Perhaps at some point today you spoke up in a meeting or had a difficult conversation with someone you love. Maybe you endured a day of illness or injury. Maybe you just made it through the day. All of these are valid and powerful battles that we fight daily. So even if right now you don't feel strong and powerful, try and hold somewhere in the back of your mind that there is great strength within you. Some days that strength will come out in amazing actions and some days it will just be you rising in the morning and going to work, and getting things done. They are all battles in their own way. Maybe today you rested because you are healing or recovering. Maybe you spent today caring for someone else. These are all victories. But as you come to the end of the day, it is time to set down your armour.

Pause

Here, at this beautiful forest clearing, you take a seat by the water's edge, taking off your shoes and dipping your feet into the water of the stream. The water trickles and sparkles over your feet and between your toes. Cool and refreshing. Washing away fatigue from your tired feet.

Here you set down your silver bow and you unclip your armour and let it fall beside you, glinting in the moonlight. You feel a little lighter for setting down this heaviness you have carried through the day. The things you have needed to achieve, they are done for now. It is time for you to rest in this space of green and calm. Perhaps you can smell on the night air the pine needles, lush green ferns, the earthy scent of soil and moss, and maybe on the gentle breeze, the floral scent of night-blooming jasmine and honeysuckle.

The moon shines a light on the water beneath you, and it sparkles gently, casting a cool light on your surroundings so that you can see the great trees and plants around you. The space is quiet and calm, you feel warm and comfortable here, connected to nature. Reconnecting to the Earth and slowing down, as you transition from day to evening and into the night.

Pause

As you rest here, letting the final layers of the day fall away, feeling calm and content, you notice to your side a little rustle in the trees and leaves beside you. So peacefully, an animal gently appears by your side and looks into your eyes. Their eyes are kind. And it may be, as you look upon this animal, whatever this animal may be in your mind's eye, they may have a message for you that you hear as you look upon them, or the message may be the symbol of the animal itself. This could be your message for this evening. Or perhaps this animal simply invites you to rest within nature, within the beauty of the natural world in the animal kingdom. A kindness and love pass between you. And this animal offers a final glance towards you as they drift back into the woods, between the trees, onwards on their own journey. As you take a few peaceful minutes in your woodland space of calm, take time to reflect upon the space around you. The day that is now done. And the evening and rest that lie ahead.

Pause

As our time in our woodland retreat comes to an end, feel free to just stay as you are, restful and calm: a warrior who is taking their time to surrender. Take the rest you have truly earned today. As you come back to the world for the rest of your evening, feel free to gently wiggle your fingers and toes, and stretch your body if you wish. When you are ready to do so, gently open your eyes and as you move through your evening, beautiful warrior, be kind and calm. Take time to enjoy your evening and your warm and restful home. It is very well earned. Thank you for joining me, warriors.

Leaving the Day Behind

This meditation is intended to help you unwind from your day and move into a restful evening. Ritual and meditation are very personal practices, so we might all take this meditation a little differently. You might use it as you come in from work and you want to take a little time to unwind, or you might use it last thing at night before you go to bed. Whichever works for you, take some time to consciously step over this threshold, and really embrace the potential for restfulness in the calm and quiet of the evening.

Take your time to settle in your own way. If you just got in, you might want to take off your shoes, you might want to get rid of any work clothes that aren't comfortable. Maybe wrap yourself in a blanket or a dressing gown, perhaps dim any bright overhead lights and light some candles. Take your time to create your evening space. Create a little sanctuary just for yourself. And when you feel ready to do so, settle into a comfortable place. And just as we take a little time to settle here, we'll say goodbye to the day and count some of the gratitudes we've experienced.

Pause

As we step over the threshold into the evening, into the night, let's first reflect on the day. We might start with simple gratitude that we had clean clothes to put on this morning; that we woke up in our warm bed; that we have food in our bellies from a day of eating breakfast, lunch, and dinner, perhaps. And then we'll move on to the people we met today.

And even some challenges we may have overcome. Maybe we are simply grateful that we made it through the day, sometimes that's enough. Take your time just to reflect on the day in gratitude for a few moments here.

Pause

Something we can always be grateful for through each day and each night is our breath. It is a constant companion. So that's where we'll move our attention next. If it's comfortable to do so, rest your hands somewhere on the chest or the tummy where you can feel the rise and fall of the breath underneath your hands. Feeling that movement, that rhythm of the breath underneath the hands and also the weight and warmth of the hands upon your body. Connecting to body and breath. That which we can always be grateful for. This body and breath that have carried us through our day.

Body and breath can now help ease us into the evening. Feeling that movement of the breath, we will inhale for a slow count of three. And exhale for a slow count of three. Taking our time. Visualising the lungs completely filling with air on that slow three count and completely emptying of air on that slow three count. And we'll continue this slow and easeful breath, a gentle rhythm. You can keep the hands on your body if that feels nice or you can just let the hands fall to a restful place.

Along with bringing all focus inwards towards that slow and steady breath, we're taking our time to consciously draw our mind towards the breath. And as we draw it inwards, we can draw our thoughts, our attention, our awareness away from our day, leaving the deadlines and schedules at our workplace.

We are consciously stepping away from the tasks we've done today, the projects, the things that have gone well and the things that have not.

Whatever has happened today, it is time now to set those things aside. Time now to embrace the here and now. The restful dark of the evening, a time for drawing inwards, for rest and reflection. As we let go of the busyness of the day.

If we've had a stressful day, we may have gathered tension within our tummy or hips. If we felt anxious, we may have felt it within our shoulders. Here is a time where we can consciously let go of those areas of the body we've been holding onto today. We've held ourselves tall. We've held ourselves strong. Now it is safe to let go. To let the body surrender. To release and allow the body to relax. Softening the feet and the legs that have carried us around today. Softening the hips and tummy. And the chest as it rises and falls with the breath. Softening the arms and shoulders, the muscles of our back. And releasing any little tensions around the neck or the jaw, or even that we may be carrying within our face in the tiny muscles around the eyes and the forehead.

We can thank the body for all that is done for us today, and how strong it has been to carry us through the day. But now it is time to bring body, breath and mind to a slower pace. An unwinding and unravelling of tension as we move into our evening. And as we take our final few minutes to relax here.

Pause

I'd like you to envisage, in your mind's eye, how you may journey from day to night. Perhaps you'll envisage stepping over the threshold of a beautiful doorway and then closing the door behind you on the stresses of the day. Maybe you walk over a bridge, a stream trickles below you, carrying away the noise of the day. Maybe you swim through water and the water washes away the day. Allow yourself to envisage the threshold you're moving over in any way you wish, as you make your conscious choice to hold this beautiful evening and night in a special place, in a special way for you. Somewhere you can relax and let go and enjoy a little peace on this beautiful evening and night.

I wish you a restful night.

Sleep into Self-Love

Spend a few restful minutes sending love and gratitude to yourself as you drift to sleep. Encouraging you to rest and restore, this is a guided body scan of love and appreciation for your wonderful body. (All bodies are an amazing and glorious gift, and delightfully varied! Feel free to leave out or add in any extra bodily areas according to your needs and preferences.)

As we settle into rest, we settle into night-time, and perhaps we'll also slip into dream time, with a little extra love for ourselves. Take your time to create your glorious, comfortable space. Arrange your cushions and your pillows, your blankets and your sheets. Allow yourself to feel completely supported by the softness around you. Feel gratitude for this place of warmth and rest and that you can be here, restful, easeful and safe. Let's begin simply by taking some long, easy breaths, helping guide us into peace and into calm. And with each exhale, imagine perhaps you are letting go just a little more. Sinking into the softness beneath you.

Pause

And here, from this restful place, we'll take a little time to send some love and gratitude to our bodies, if it feels comfortable to do so. Feel free here to gently rest the hands on your body. Or you might just want to bring your mind's eye to the areas of your lower body: your legs, your knees, your ankles.

○ Allow your awareness, for just a moment, to hover above the feet and ankles. Thank your feet for allowing you to root into the earth. To stand strong, to stand in your power. Even when you don't feel that powerful, your feet are still there rooting into the earth, providing you your strong foundation.

○ We bring our attention to our legs, our knees, our strong thighs. Thank your legs for allowing you to stand tall. Sometimes we feel unsure. Sometimes we feel fearful. But your legs keep you standing strong. They allow you to walk and run and jump and swim. Sometimes they may be tired, sometimes they may ache. But your legs support you all the same.

○ Next, we send a little love to our beautiful hips that allow us to move and sway with music, to find a balance, to steady ourselves in strong winds. Our hips give us the freedom of movement and allow us to find our flow. Thank you, hips.

o We send love and gratitude to our legs and lower body.

o As we move up our body, maybe lay the hands on your tummy, your chest or heart. Anywhere in the centre of your body that feels nice, or simply bring your awareness to this area.

o Sending love to our beautiful tummies. Soft and warm. Feel how your tummy and chest rise and fall with the breath. Tummy and chest. Your very centre. Your very core. Housing all your organs. Allowing you to be your wonderful self. Within that chest beats your beautiful heart. It may have had some knocks and scrapes along your journey. But it beats strong. It beats steady. It allows you to love and be loved. It allows you to go forth into this world and be a force of beautiful, gorgeous love. Thank you, heart.

o Allow your attention now to sweep over your shoulders, arms, elbows and hands. These beautiful limbs that allow us to wave, to gesture, to create beautiful shapes in dance, in movement and create things in craft. Thank you, beautiful arms and beautiful hands.

o Allow your attention to sweep through your neck and throat and jaw. Thank these beautiful spaces for allowing you to speak your truth, to sing, to call, to be heard.

o And finally, we allow our attention to sweep over our face and eyes and the very top of our heads. Our eyes that allow us to see the world in all its beauty. Our mind's eye, our third eye chakra, rests between the eyebrows and allows us to see the beauty within ourselves.

○ Here we send love and gratitude to our entire body. This marvellous miracle body, that allows us to live our lives, dancing and singing. And as we rest in this comfortable place, we thank our body and allow it now time to rest. To sink, to settle and to surrender.

Pause

It is time, my darlings, to embrace the body with love. And sink into rest. May your dreams be sweet, and your love be endless.

JOURNEYING WITH THE DIVINE AND SACRED

We can all of us meet and be inspired by archetypes of the divine feminine and divine masculine. Whilst learning and reading about classical archetypes of deities is wonderful, there is also something very special about meeting them in meditation, in a space of intuition. You may use these 'divine' meditations as days of consecutive journey, or select deities that you are particularly drawn to.

We will explore some sacred spaces, from the library to the forest, the cauldron and the temple, to the wildflower meadow. In our mind's eye we can travel wherever we wish! And in these places we may find wisdom and learning, release and forgiveness, or strength and fortitude, such is the magic of sacred space.

The Divine Feminine

The Maiden

The archetype of the Maiden connects to feelings of youthfulness and hope. Within the Maiden archetype, you'll find qualities of excitement for the new, and a joy in the possibility of life that perhaps we felt as young children. Many goddesses, especially those of spring and dawn, are portrayed in young maiden form, such as Artemis, who runs through the woods with her bow and arrows, unhindered by concerns and authority figures telling her what to do.

The Maiden represents hopefulness, innocence, and joy in nature and in the elements. And certainly, when we're thinking about how archetypes mirror elements of ourselves, the Maiden is one that we can lose track of sometimes. We might call this connecting to our inner child – reconnecting to joy we perhaps felt when we were younger and unconstrained by adult responsibilities.

We'll prepare for our meditation, as always, taking as long as we need to find a comfortable place, a restful place. Allow the body to begin to relax. Slowing and settling the breath to help guide the body into restfulness and calm. Preparing to let the physical body rest as we take our journey through the mind's eye.

Pause

Imagine that you are walking through a beautiful spring meadow. The sun is warm on your skin. And you feel the softness of the grass beneath your feet. Allow all of your senses to absorb your environment. You may feel the warmth of the sunshine upon your skin or the kiss of a gentle breeze. You may smell grass or the gentle scent of flowers on the air. You may hear leaves and branches rustling in the breeze or the sound of birdsong in the distance. Allow yourself to take in this beautiful sunny springtime meadow, this beautiful space in nature. And see the potential in the space around you, the shoots of some plants are just starting to come back to life in the spring season.

As you continue to walk over this meadow space, you see before you a sea of spring wildflowers in every single colour, shape and size you can imagine. They might be real flowers that mean something to you: primroses, daisies, poppies, daffodils, violets, or they might be flowers that you have never seen before. Amazing colours, sparkling and shining in the light. And as you gaze over these beautiful flowers, you notice that each one represents something to you. It may be that the colour and shape of the flower means something to you, or it might be that there are physical words floating on or around the flowers. Each and every one of these beautiful flowers represents a hope or a dream that you have somewhere within your heart or your consciousness. These hopes and dreams can be as simple as to be happy, to feel safe, to be content. Or as detailed as wishing to train to be a vet, or to travel to a certain country, or to dye your hair a certain colour. Any dream or goal that you have ever held exists within this wildflower meadow! And as you allow these ideas and dreams to swirl around your mind with excitement and hopefulness, you begin to create a beautiful bouquet of flowers. You pick the flowers that bring you most joy or most excitement, or simply because they're the ones that speak to you right now. So take your time, create your wildflower dream bouquet. And when your beautiful bouquet is ready, when you're happy with it, just take a moment to drink in the colours, drink in the hope and excitement that this bouquet represents for you. And feel free to channel the maiden goddesses, the maiden aspects of any goddess or being that speaks to you.

Pause

The Maiden represents freedom, hope and looking at life without the cynicism that sometimes we gather as we grow older. Maybe you even imagine your inner child speaking to you as you look upon these flowers. What would they say, how excited would they be by this beautiful collection of dreams?

Pause

And when the time comes, when you know it's time to leave this beautiful meadow, you take a final look at your beautiful bouquet. Taking in the beauty, the hope and the dreams within. And then you place the bunch of flowers back onto the earth, back onto the grass of the meadow… All at once each flower, each stem, reconnects back to the earth. Once again, the flowers live, and they are here now, so that they can continue to grow. Each one of your dreams, each one of your hopes, is still here, still growing, still tended by your love and light. So you feel hopeful and full of excitement as you leave this beautiful meadow, knowing that the flowers are here for you always.

As the time comes to bring your awareness back to the world, feel free to take your time to gently stretch and move. Maybe wiggle the fingers and toes. And whenever you feel ready to do so, gently open the eyes and bring yourself back to the room. Welcome back!

Journaling Ideas

Take your time to sit with these ideas of your hopes and dreams, or you can note and draw the flowers and dreams down if you wish. I would love you to put this list or drawing up somewhere where you can see it, maybe near a place where you work or where you meditate, just so that that little hope, that little sparkle carried within the Maiden's energy can remind you that we all have hopes. We all have dreams. Some we will realise. Some maybe not. But even having these dreams and goals can bring us joy and excitement just to remind ourselves how many possibilities there are in the world. And we may remember when we were young, when everything and anything seemed possible. I want you to remind yourself of that as often as you can.

The Oracle

Today's archetype is that of the Oracle. The name of those re-lated to foreseeing or gaining insight or reading sacred signs is Sybil. And this name has been applied to special women throughout history. The Sybil's gift of prophecy links her to the divine. She acts as a medium between us and the divine. She also reminds us that the ability to be intuitive, to connect and recognise signs and symbols is something that is within us all. This is not an ability left to just one goddess, one deity, but something that we can all embrace, something that is innate to us. And it may be that over time we've become disconnected from our ability to read the signs within ourselves of our own bodies, our own patterns of energy, and the signs of the world around us. But this ability has not been lost. It is always with-in us. Sometimes we just need a little time to reconnect.

We'll get ourselves settled for our meditation. Taking as long as we wish to gather blankets or cushions and find a comfort-able place to settle. As we relax the body, we relax the mind and allow the breath to become easy, calm and unhurried. Ar-riving into a place of settling, a place of softening, a place of letting go. Imagine busy thoughts swirling out of the mind, like whirls of smoke or incense. Allow the body to sink into stillness.

Pause

We find ourselves in our mind's eye in the seclusion and darkness of a cave. Great walls of rock surround us. On each uneven surface rest candles: tiny tea lights, great pillar candles, candles in jars of many colours. The cave is aglow with warming light, plumes of incense, smoke hanging in the air. At the centre of the cave rests a great low metal dish filled with flames and smoke. As you approach the flames, you hear the voices of all Sybils from all ages. A line of divine women. They have been waiting for you. Their prophecies of years past hang gently in the incense-filled air.

They are caught in the flickers of the candles around you. The voices of the Sybils remind you that theirs were not the only voices of the Goddess. They, just like you, sat by a flame and waited. They gazed into the swirling smoke and hoped to hear the voice of the Goddess. All souls possess the gift to connect to the Goddess. Because she is within us all. So, as you gaze upon the flames and smoke in this cave of peacefulness, allow yourself to see what you see. Whatever it may be or nothing at all. Allow yourself to visualise the smoke and the flames. And connect to any messages the deities, or the universe may have for you today in this moment.

Pause

And the time comes, just for now, for you to leave this sacred cave, this dark and quiet place. Know that you can return to this place any time. You may return here in your mind's eye.

Take your time to stretch, unfurl and unravel. Take some nice deep breaths and maybe wiggle the fingers and toes. You can stay here, as always, as long as you wish, simply to process what you have seen or thought or anything that has come up in your meditation today. Feel free to note down anything you have seen or thought in words or images.

Journaling Ideas

As you move through your days and the seasons, take a little time, just to notice things around you. You may want to note them down: the number of birds you see in the sky, the flowers you may come across, the animals that cross your path. These can all be messages, divine symbols, connections to your life and the rhythm of your energy. I'm not saying that everything you come across has to be a message or that it has to mean something. But it's possible to connect to our powerful intuition and insight in these simple, tiny moments of magic in the day. So, if something catches your eye or causes you pause, make a note of it. You can write it down in your note-book or just take a mental note and maybe reflect on it later on what it may mean for you. In this way, in simple little ways, we can always connect to our inner oracle.

The Queen

In today's meditation, we will explore the divine feminine archetype of the Queen. The Queen reminds us that we all deserve to be cherished and respected as sovereign. As Queens of our domain, we are worshipped and respected. But also, we have to make challenging decisions, whether it be for the good of our family, our work team or tribe of any kind: with the power of the Queen comes responsibility. This meditation is about the powerful feminine, and feeling empowered to take steps towards what we want.

Embracing this archetype of the Queen, we'll get ready for our guided meditation today. Take your time to get comfortable and relax. Allow yourself to settle and soften. Allow yourself to let go of tension or tightness.

Pause

Our guided meditation today will be about creating a life we love with the power of our Queen archetype. Drawing on an understanding that loving ourselves is the most essential prerequisite to living our best life. When we feel good and powerful about who we are, we radiate energy. We naturally make good choices because we feel deserving of our best lives, our lives as Queens or sovereigns.

As you settle into this meditation, give yourself permission to connect with your deepest desires. Allow a vision of yourself at your highest and happiest to form within your mind. Perhaps bring to mind the area of your life that you most want to improve or transform. This may be an area of your life that has caused you struggle or where you're seeking fulfilment. This area may be relationships, career, finances, family… Allow yourself to acknowledge for now just one area that you wish to transform, to attend to, to nurture and nourish with your attention. Allow yourself to create an intention: a vision for this part of your life. Allow yourself to visualise this area of your life exactly as you wish it to be. Envisage yourself experiencing this element of your life. You might picture what you're wearing or where you are, the emotions you're feeling, your interactions with others. Allow yourself to visualise it exactly as you wish it to be.

Focus on the emotions you feel when you are living your

best life: you may feel joy, you may feel empowered. You may simply feel free of stress. Now, allow yourself to think of when you have previously experienced or displayed these qualities. If confidence and joy are what you wish to bring into this area of your life, recall a time in your life when you have expressed confidence or joyfulness. Imagine a circumstance under which you have felt confident. And allow yourself to feel how these qualities that you know you want to develop already exist within you. You are already capable of finding joy, of finding confidence, you can feed your attention and intention to these qualities.

Now, look again at that ideal life, that particular area. Can you bring the qualities that you have shown in the past to this time? Can you bring the strength you have displayed in the past to create your ideal life? Can you bring the love, the patience, the confidence, the joy? Can you bring it to the here and now and apply it to this new idea, this new journey towards developing within the area you wish to grow? And now just allow yourself to see how this area of your life may be different if you embrace the qualities you possess whenever you want them. Imagine perhaps how you would feel or what you would plan to accomplish, how people around you would respond to you and let's just breathe with that.

Pause

So, when you feel ready, you may wish to gently wiggle your fingers and toes as we begin to leave our meditation today. And as always, you may wish to just sit here with your thoughts and reflect on this meditation, or you may wish to take up your notepad and pen.

Journaling Ideas

If you do wish to write after this meditation, we're going to reflect on how we can allow ourselves to put into place and nurture the qualities you identified to help you on your journey, or grow in this area of your life. Maybe think on what you can do daily, weekly or monthly to encourage these qualities to shine in full force in your life. For example, if you identified courage as something that would enable you to create your vision, what can you do on a daily basis to nurture and foster courage within you? Take your time to reflect on the qualities you've identified. And on how you can nurture or nourish these qualities so that you can be the sovereign you were born to be. As always, take as long as you wish to write or draw or to simply rest with your thoughts.

The Healer

Welcome to this meditation on the archetype of the Healer. Here we will reflect on our own power to heal ourselves: to heal with love, to heal with forgiveness, to nourish ourselves. Feeling well in ourselves is freedom. Feeling well-rested, well-nourished, and knowing that we are truly looking after our body and mind allows us freedom. It's the greatest form of abundance we can enjoy. This is also a reminder that we can honour our own wellness and healing by acknowledging our own cycles and rhythms by listening to what the body needs as it changes from day to day and year to year.

With this in mind, in this honouring of ourselves, our rhythms and our need for rest, we will prepare to move into our meditation today. So, as always, we'll take time to find a restful and comfortable place as we allow the body and breath to relax.

Pause

In your mind's eye you are surrounded by mist. Swirling mist envelops your body. You may imagine this mist as a colour. It may contain stars or sparkles. This mist can look however you wish, as it surrounds you, feeling warm upon your skin, carrying a gentle scent of flowers and herbs. The mist is thick, and you can no longer see your surroundings. This is a chance for you to let go of whatever sort of day you have had, whatever worries you carry with you, let them fall away here into the mist. As you rest, as if floating within a cloud, feeling restful and calm, you notice that there is a glowing light very close to you. In your mind's eye, you rise from your resting place.

The mist clears a little and you see there is a space that has been surrounded by candles. Each one gently flickering through the haze. The space looks very warm and inviting. So, you walk over to this place.

Surrounded by the flickering candles and warm lights is a large copper bathtub. This is where the steam, the mist, has been rising from. And now the mist has cleared a little, you can see things more clearly. It is a beautiful space. The bathtub rests in the centre of a room with candles and incense burning on every surface. Surrounding the bathtub are four beautiful women. They are preparing a concoction within the bathtub from which the scents and steam are rising.

These four women coming to your vision may be women that you know and love. They may be four goddesses. They may be angels or fairies or simply four kind women with whom you feel safe. They work easefully, as if performing a dance. Finding herbs and petals from shelves and jars, they scatter rose petals upon the water. They stir in jasmine flowers. They cast sprigs of lavender and rosemary into the water. Stirring this beautiful cauldron as the steam rises in whirls of colour and scent. As you approach the bathtub and the women, they smile: they have been expecting you.

One of the women holds out her arms and you gently lay your clothes upon her hands so that she can put them somewhere safe. The other women guide you towards the bath. You dip your toes into the water. It is the perfect temperature – warm and soothing – and you sink into the bath water, allowing your entire body to be enveloped by water, steam, colour and scent.

The women give you one last smile, seeing that you are settled and happy, they step back, disappearing into the mist. You feel the warmth, the soothing of the water upon your body as if the gentle, healing powers of this bath, of this cauldron of healing magic, are sinking into your bones, your muscles, your joints. You feel soothed and nourished, and happy to simply bask in this place. The warmth eases tensions and tightness. Worries and concerns or thoughts that are moving around in your mind gently drift away, like the steam rising from the water. And maybe, as you sink a little deeper into the bath water, you feel comfortable to let your head drop under the waterline. So that you are completely immersed in the water and the world goes very quiet. Just for a moment, you are suspended in warmth and colour. Just for a moment, suspended in a perfect place of warm water.

And as your head gently rises above the waterline once more you take a deep breath and exhale. Feeling as though you have washed your body clean of tension and tightness, the fatigue of anxiety and stress. You have nourished your body with warmth and love and time to just be.

You feel peaceful as the time comes to leave your beautiful bath. There is a large, warm, fluffy robe waiting for you, left by one of the women. As you rise, wrapping yourself in your cosy robe you feel refreshed, recharged, and nourished and ready to move forward on your healing journey. This is just the beginning. Of caring for yourself. For your beautiful body, your beautiful mind and your beautiful heart.

Pause

When you feel ready to do so, gently open your eyes and move the body or stretch or twist if you wish to as you take a little time to bring yourself back to the room, back to the world. You may wish to just rest here as we come away from our meditation.

Journaling Ideas

If you wish to do so, you can take up your pen and paper and take some time to reflect on what is healing for you. It may be something as simple as taking a bath and taking some rest time for yourself. It may be nourishing your body with foods you know are healing and nutritious. It may be taking time to speak to your friends and family or in-depth work with a professional. You may find that time spent in nature, in forests or by the ocean, feel healing for you.

Whether you are in good physical health or if you are recovering from an illness or an operation, or there are chronic issues that you work with, there is always an opportunity for you to bring your own healing magic to yourself. Think about how you can use your energy on yourself to help make any situation you're in a little more healing, a little more nourishing. Do the best you can do for yourself so that you can go forward feeling just a little stronger, a little more well, a little more settled and abundant in your own heart and your own self. Take as long as you wish to make your list and reflect upon what you can do to help yourself heal in whatever form that may take, physical, emotional or spiritual.

The Crone

In today's meditation, we'll be embracing the divine feminine archetype of the Crone. Working with the Crone is so interesting for many reasons, but particularly in today's society where growing older can be a source of fear and trepidation. We don't always look forward to growing older physically and the challenges that may befall us in many aspects of our lives as we age. However, just like the phases of the Moon, with each one holding its own beauty, as we grow older and inhabit our cronehood, we can find wisdom, peace, and acceptance. We find wisdom from the things we learn, from life experiences and accumulated knowledge. We can find peace as we let go of pressures around performance or any ideals of success or worrying about trivial matters. Perhaps we become just a little less affected by the dramas of the world. Perhaps we develop a beautiful acceptance of who we really are and what our dreams and goals are. Perhaps we no longer feel like we have to fit into moulds or shapes that society would dictate. Now is the time to inhabit who we truly are. As a reflective practice I recommend this as a meditation for the end of the day.

***Please note:** I do touch briefly on grief and loss near the end of this meditation. Please bear this in mind if you (or anyone you are leading in meditation) are working with these things right now. This meditation may prove useful for release and reflection, but if you feel you are not in the right place to journey with these ideas today, however gently, perhaps revisit this journey another time.*

We'll prepare for our meditation. Take your time to find a warm and comfortable place to sit or lie. Create a space that can nourish, nurture and comfort you at this time. Whenever you feel ready, you can close your eyes as you allow the body to soften and relax into the earth. Allow the breath to fall into a slow and gentle rhythm.

Pause

In our mind's eye, we journey outside into a world covered in white. We walk over a great meadow covered in pure white snow. Allow the view of this white expanse to fill your mind. In the distance, rolling hills, snow-topped trees and mountains can be seen. The snow is pure and white, and as you walk softly on the snow, yours are the first footprints upon it. As you take in your surroundings, the blankets of white covering the world you see before you, you notice that you are robed in white. Beautiful, soft, warm clothing, all bright white.

You notice your hair that falls about your shoulders is also as white and pure as the snow around you. You complement the environment you're in, as if you were born to be here, at home in the snow. A bright being of light. And as you stand in the snow looking behind you, you see so clearly each and every one of your footsteps. Each and every one of the steps you have taken to the exact spot you are right now. And as you reflect on these footsteps, you may see symbols or plants or animals that represent memories to you. Each step may represent a year or a place or an adventure that means something to you and who you are. Take a minute or two simply to reflect on the steps that have brought you to this moment.

Pause

And now from our place in the snow, we'll turn from looking backwards at our footsteps, to looking forward to those rolling hills, the mountains and treetops, beautiful and glistening with snow and frost.

Take a few more minutes here to reflect on the journey ahead. A journey for which there is no path. You may move forward in any direction you please. You may move forward with a strong idea of where you are heading; to the mountains, to the trees. You may move forward without knowing and simply enjoy the journey. Maybe a little bit of both. But as you reflect on the steps you've taken and are inspired by the journey yet to come, you feel good that you have made it this far.

You have gathered wisdom and knowledge on every single step you have taken. So wherever the oncoming path leads, you are looking forward to it.

All of us, whatever our age, can learn from the archetype of the Crone, the acceptance of who we are, the accumulated wisdom. We can never know for certain which route we're taking and where it will lead us. Sometimes choices have to be made. And in such cases, the way to nurture wholeness is to trust in your knowledge. Trust in yourself. And whichever path you choose, step into it with your whole being. Walk confidently in that direction because any path you choose, when you bring your own strength and power to it, can be the right path.

And as we explore the process of growing older, whether we are in our Crone aspect now or simply journeying towards it, we will lose things. We may lose ideas and passions, we may lose physical elements of ourselves, whether it's the colour of

78

our hair or the thinness of our waistline. Things will come and go. We will lose people to time. We will all love, and we will all grieve. So hold on to gratitude for the things we have while we are honoured to have them.

Pause

As the time comes to return from our place in the snow, take a few long, deep breaths, as we gently and easefully bring ourselves back to the room. As we come to the end of this meditation, you may just wish to stay with your thoughts and reflect on this meditation or return to your day after some time to regroup.

Journaling Ideas

You may wish to make note of your fears around ageing and growing older. But also reflect on what you will gain on the journey, as all things have balance. This can also be useful to help arrange priorities, values and ideas.

The Divine Masculine

The Green Man

In today's meditation, we will journey with the spirit of the natural world, a symbol of the woodland and the forest: the Green Man. The image of the Green Man (or sometimes Green Woman) is that of a face haloed with leaves, a representation of nature and the natural world. It is often found carved into church stonework in the British Isles, and is a vibrant figure in our folklore. Most often we see the face encircled by leaves of oak, a symbol of strength, endurance, and power. And it is with this simple but powerful image that we will journey in meditation today.

Take your time to find yourself somewhere that is comfortable, warm and supported. Take as long as you need. When you are ready, you can close your eyes. And take some time to breathe. Breathe so that you may find an easeful rhythm, a pace with which to find a little peacefulness. Breathe so that you may relax your body. It might be that each exhale is a letting go of any tension or tightness you may be holding onto. And breathe so that you may bring your awareness towards that rhythm of the breath and away from any busy thoughts and to-do lists or schedules, any noises from the outside world.

This is our time to journey inwards, to connect to the beautiful world of nature and green spaces using the power of meditation and the mind. All we need do is breathe and relax.

Pause

Within the mind, let us envisage the beauty of the natural world. You may find yourself with bare feet upon warm, lush grass. You may be wearing your favourite hiking boots and walking a scenic trail. You may find yourself in a woodland clearing, in a meadow, wildwood or forest. Take your time to visualize this place that may come from memory or imagination. Beautiful shades of green surround you in grass and leaf and flower and plant. Beyond tall canopies of trees the sky is bright and blue. The warmth and light of the sun scatters through leaves and branches. Or perhaps it is shining bright upon an open meadow. We take in the sensations of the space around us: light and warmth and colour. The solidity of the ground beneath us.

This, as all realms of nature are, is the world of the Green

Man. The Green One, the spirit of the natural world, is watching over us here. Keeping a quiet protective eye. As you connect to this place, and become more and more part of it, you feel a sensation of your feet running deep into the earth, strong roots finding their grounding. Your body so strong and tall. Like the tree trunk of the great oak tree. Rising. Rising towards the sun.

You may feel that you want to – either in your mind's eye or through your physical body – reach out the arms and stretch all the way through your fingertips. Like beautiful branches sweeping in the wind, you can reach wide, you can reach skywards. Allowing the strength of your roots and tree trunk to give you that support to expand in every way. And finally that beautiful halo of oak leaves might expand out from your branches, your arms, hands and fingers. It might shine out from your heart, chest and shoulders as we see in depictions of the Green Man.

The bright spray of oak leaves shines out from you in a beautiful aura. You are the Green One. The Green One is you. And just as every other oak tree does in this beautiful place of nature, you will feel your roots. Trust in the strength of your core and stretch out and up towards the sun.

Pause

I invite you, dear one, to gently wiggle your fingers and toes, maybe wiggle your arms and legs. We might imagine this movement is gently letting go of each one of those oak leaves from our body, casting them away to be carried into a warm breeze and once again returned to the Earth. We might wiggle our hips and shoulders to begin to move the spine and torso. Our great tall tree trunk finding movement and ease. And maybe flex your feet, drawing up your energy from those beautiful roots back to your body here in this room.

Pause

Just before you leave that green space in the mind's eye, feel free to take a moment to send your thanks and gratitude to the natural world. To the Green Man. To the spirit of this place. When you feel ready to do so, take a nice big stretch and a nice deep breath.

Gently open the eyes and I will welcome you back. Thank you so much for joining me and the spirit of nature on this journey today.

Cernunnos

In today's journey of meditation, we will walk deep into the wild wood and find wonder as we meet with an ancient god. He is the Celtic god, Cernunnos,* though he goes by many names, as do all our most ancient deities who journey through time and texts and cultures. Cernunnos, as the symbol of the great stag, is often depicted with great antlers upon his head. In ancient cultures, the symbol of the stag, of the horned one, represents, among other things, power and sovereignty.

---

*   Pronounced *CARE-noo-nos*

We begin in safety and sanctuary. Take your time to relax. Find your restful place and close your eyes. Wrap yourself up in blankets, warm and restful, breathing easily. You are safe here, supported, as you envisage your body here in its place upon the ground.

We'll take a sweep of awareness. We take our time as we bring our awareness to our toes; allow them to soften and relax. Now, the legs, the knees and the kneecaps relax as we let go of these tensions of the body. We soften the hips and tummy and chest. Allow the shoulders to relax. They have carried great weight through the day, and now they can soften. Take your wave of awareness through the arms and down to the tips of the fingers. Relaxing peacefully. And finally, that wave of awareness and mindfulness moves up through your neck and your jaw all the way to the top of your head. Allow your whole body to relax.

In this place of restfulness and calm, we find ourselves now not lying in the place we started, but now we rest in wild woodland. Soft and supported, on grass or moss. It is dark around you, but you feel calm. There is a sense of peacefulness glowing within your heart. In fact, that glowing of light within you feels almost as if it grows and shines out from you. Maybe it is your eyes growing accustomed to the dark. Maybe it is the sun rising in the east. But this shining light allows you now to see a little lighter and brighter around you. You are aware now of trees and plants. Tall and elegant around you. And now, not just trees and plants, but a figure. A horned man approaches you. He's wearing a great cape made of a patchwork of moss, and trousers patterned in browns that match the trees. You know immediately that this figure with his grand horns, his beautiful antlers, is Cernunnos. He approaches you with a soft smile. He sits down beside you. You take a moment to sit together and enjoy the view.

And then quick and calm, like a stag rising from resting, Cernunnos gets to his feet and draws you up with him. You move swiftly, silently through the forest. He wishes to show you a beautiful throne made of branches and bark, and he sits upon this throne. To his left, is a fox, beautiful with a sleek coat of gold and orange and bright eyes. Perched just above his shoulder, a black raven, also bright-eyed. With great wings, he flies gently from his perch and sits upon your shoulder. The raven and Cernunnos seem to say without words: *you are safe here, child.* And you find yourself nodding gently: you do feel safe in this place. You feel held within the strength and power of the natural world. And with that same benevolent smile, Cernunnos turns and shows you…yourself. You have not moved from your resting place upon the moss, you have journeyed with him in spirit. You have been resting in meditation this whole time. Discovering this liminal space. A portal between worlds. You may both be resting and running through trees all at once.

As the raven flies back to his perch upon the throne, you bid farewell to your forest friends and this little adventure into a world beyond worlds. They wish you farewell and remind you that they will always be here, should you ever wish to journey through the realm simply to be amongst them: the trees in peace, the god upon his throne, the animals of the wood. They are always here for you. Watching. Ready to guide, should you need it. Within the woodland, there is such magic to be found and we can journey back any time we wish within our mind's eye or as we take a walk in nature. To remind ourselves of the magic we can see. And of the magic we can't see.

And as you find your awareness drawing back into your body that lies in the woodland upon the moss and the grass, your awareness also comes back to your body in the here and now. You bring your awareness back to the day. You can open your eyes and I welcome you back to the world.

Sacred Spaces

Rainbow Chakra Wildflowers

In this meditation each of the chakras of the body is represented with colourful wildflowers. A sunny meadow, a field of flowers, and a bright sky to bring you through this meditation – a journey of light and colour! I'll be describing each of the seven chakras, the energy centres of the body, but you do not need any knowledge of the chakras to enjoy this meditation.

Letting the body relax as we settle, let the muscles soften, the limbs be heavy.

In our mind's eye we're going to take a little journey. Envisage yourself in a beautiful green field or meadow. Beneath you, soft green grass that has been warmed by the sun supports you gently. Above you, a great blue sky sweeps from horizon to horizon. Maybe we imagine that any thoughts or distractions we have are little clouds in the sky, and we'll just gently let them drift from our view so that we are left with a beautiful, clear blue sky. Can we allow all of our senses to bring us to this beautiful place?

We feel the grass beneath us. And maybe the warmth of a beautiful, bright sun somewhere up in the blue sky. Maybe we feel the kiss of a warm breeze upon our cheeks. Maybe we smell the grass and the scent of wildflowers on the breeze. Maybe we hear the gentle sounds of grass rustling. Allow yourself to use all of your senses to find yourself within this meadow, within this place of nature that is so calm and peaceful, warm and welcoming.

From this restful place you notice now that surrounding you are great swathes of wildflowers. In every colour of the rainbow. They gently dance in the breeze. Colours and scent whirling around you. And as a slightly stronger gust of warm breeze whips up, all at once, petals and flowers are gently whisked into the air. In a flurry of colour, these petals and flowers dance around you. And as the breeze stills, the petals drift. And some of them land upon you as you lie on your restful place upon the grass. These petals are so soft and warm. You feel joyful. Maybe even smile or laugh as these little kisses of colour find their homes resting upon you.

Firstly you become aware of a petal that has fallen upon the very top of your head. It is a beautiful violet colour. It might be a petal or a whole blossom that rests in your hair like a tiny crown. This little flower represents the crown chakra. The beautiful violet colour is a symbol of illumination and connection with the universe. This little bloom's gift to you is a message that you are connected to the energy of the universe. And you feel this message gently within you, soaking it into the top of your head and your mind in a journey of light and colour, an illumination.

The next petal is a beautiful, deep, dark blue. And it rests on your forehead just between your eyebrows, at the home of the third eye chakra. This little petal's message to you is that your mind is open, and you can feel that expanding energy.

The beautiful deep blue colour and the light and the warmth sink into this little space between your eyebrows.

The next beautiful petals rest at the base of your neck where the collar bones meet. And they are a beautiful, vibrant turquoise colour. These petals of turquoise represent the throat chakra. Our place of communication, wisdom and truth. And these little blossoms that rest at your collarbones send you blessings so that you may always be heard and may always be able to speak your truth.

The next petals are a beautiful bright green. They come to rest at the heart: our heart centre and heart chakra. Their beautiful green mirrors the life around us, the grass and the trees and the leaves. Here, with these petals, we find ourselves at the meeting point between heaven and earth: the centre of our being, a place of compassion and peace. May you always attune to the frequency of love.

The next beautiful flower petals rest just above your belly button and are such a vibrant yellow, they seem to reflect the light and sparkle of the sun. This place of light is our solar plexus chakra. A home of energy, determination and enthusiasm: our own inner sunshine. The rays of your inner sun shine out to meet the rays of the sun above you. Perhaps, in your mind's eye, you say to yourself: *I am peaceful. I am powerful. I shine with the light of the sun.*

The next beautiful blossoms that rest just below the belly button are a rich, warm orange. This is our sacral chakra. The home of our creative flow and joy. This beautiful energy centre allows us to connect to the flow of life, and the petals remind us so.

And the last beautiful bloom that rests upon us is at the

bottom of the pelvis, the bottom of our spine. Our root chakra. Our place of stability and grounding. A connection to the earth and our ancestors. And this beautiful wildflower of earthy red sends a message to you: *my roots support me. I am grounded and I am safe.*

Each of these beautiful flowers, these beautiful petals, that have found their home upon you bring with them warmth, light, comfort and inspiration. Allow yourself to bask in the sun, in the light, in the colour of these wild flower chakras.

And as the gentle, warm breeze picks up just a little, the flowers and petals are once more picked up by the wind. They dance around you once again before returning to the flower beds.

You may want to take some deep breaths. You may want to stretch or move your body. Basking in this light and energy you have drawn in through our meditation today. Whenever you feel ready to do so, gently open the eyes and return to the world.

The Witch and the Night Garden

In this session, I wanted to explore a little bit of moon magic with whispers of the Witch archetype. Whether we connect to this idea of being a witch or simply enjoy connecting to the archetype, harnessing the power of the Witch (and the moon) in visualisation can help us connect to our own powers and makes for some very beautiful spells and rituals. All of our ancestors would once have gazed up at that silvery glow in the night sky and tried to make sense of its rhythms, and all of us can connect to a little magic on moonlit nights.

Let's create a soft and safe place to rest. Find a space where you can relax and be warm and feel safe. Allow the cares of the day, the ideas and anything else that's jumping around in your mind to drift away. And the body relaxes.

Our journey tonight will take us to a magical night garden. You visualise yourself standing barefoot upon soft grass. A great circular archway is in front of you, a doorway. Completely circular, it is known as a moon gate. Wound around the moon gate are beautiful white roses, intertwined with jasmine and moon flowers, which are so bright and white that they sparkle, reflecting the moon in the night sky above you. The scent of these flowers is beautiful, soft and welcoming, and you draw closer to the moon gate.

You are drawn to step through, and it is as though you have stepped through a portal from the day-to-day world of tasks and deadlines. We have left those things behind as we move into a garden of magic where the flowers sparkle. The scent here is so beautiful, it seems to whirl around you. And you are drawn into this magical place. Tree branches cast loving arms around and above you. Hanging from these trees are lanterns with candles within, wind chimes and bells that tinkle gently in the soft night breezes.

Perhaps you hear the hoot of a friendly owl. And maybe sense that there are magical creatures nearby, peering over snowdrops and hiding behind leaves. The friendly fairies of the garden welcome you from their safe spaces.

At the centre of this magical garden is a beautiful pool of water. The water is so clear and clean and calm that it reflects the night sky. The stars and moon sparkle in the water. You are drawn to this beautiful pool to gaze upon the reflections cast on its surface. Petals of the white roses and little jasmine blooms float upon the water. This body of water is a healing bath created just for you, and you dip your bare feet into it.

The water is warm and soothing. You descend a little deeper into the pool. You feel marble beneath your feet. As you descend into the water, let it rise up around you. Still and calm. Enveloping you in warmth like a hug. You feel the water take the weight of your body. You feel weightless in this space. And so, you lie back into the water and all becomes completely quiet. You gaze up at the stars and moon above you. Completely supported. Completely weightless. Amongst the flowers, the stars and the sparkling water. And, of course, watched over by the moon.

Drifting in this water, you feel as though a little weight has been washed away from you. A little tension released from your body. You have not cast a spell or done any ritual but this is simple ancient magic, of water cleansing away tension under the light of the moon. You feel refreshed and nourished.

As you gently rise from this pool you notice that someone or something has left a beautiful warm robe hanging from a tree branch. It is beautiful shades of silver, and it sparkles. You wrap it around you, and feel warm and cosy, nourished and somehow strengthened from your experience. As though you have washed away and let go of a few things that no longer serve you.

The time comes to leave the night garden to pass once more back through the moon gate. It is time to return to the world. But you can stay restful for as long as you wish. Perhaps a few final moments. With the flowers and the stars and the fairies of the night garden. Stay here as long as you wish. Good night, witches. May you always find a little comfort and magic in the night.

Moon Goddess Temple

Welcome to this meditation exploring some of the goddesses associated with the moon. In mythology, the moon is almost always portrayed as a woman, because the energy of the divine feminine reflects the cool, calm, intuitive nature of the moon and its cycles, but also in full knowledge that the moon can move oceans when it wishes to. It is both powerful and intuitive, strong and calm.

Let's journey into meditation, and maybe we'll meet a few of those moon goddesses. Let's allow ourselves to relax in a space that is warm, comfortable, and safe. You can close the eyes or let the gaze be soft as we begin to relax into our space.

Peaceful and unhurried breaths. Letting the limbs soften and allowing the breath to guide us to a place of calm and peace. You are safe to relax in this space.

Pause

In our mind's eye, we find ourselves standing in front of a great marble temple. Vast columns rise up to support a large roof. You note a beautiful glass dome on top of this roof that must open up towards the sky. As your eyes travel upwards, you see the stars sparkling above you: night-time is here. The temple is well-lit with flaming torches and candles. Oil lamps burn, casting golden light over this temple of the goddess.

In ancient cultures, people created the goddesses using things they knew, to explain things they did not. They drew the best elements of themselves as humans: strength, passion, intuition and knowledge, and created the archetypes of the great goddesses. So, when we connect to the energy of the goddess, we are really connecting to energy of ourselves, power that is within us. The goddess can inspire us to reconnect and find strength.

You are excited by this possibility as you walk up the steps of the temple and through the great tall doors. You move into the temple space. You find more lights and candles lighting up the room. Bowls of incense burn and scent drifts around the space. As you move into the central room of the temple, you look up and once more notice that great glass oculus through which, just as you predicted, you can see the night sky. The space around you is beautiful. There are bowls of shining red grapes, figs and olives. In the corner, musicians play gentle music. The atmosphere is calm but joyful.

A beautiful woman in a silver robe gently touches your arm. She smiles and guides you to a bench covered in silver material and beautiful plump pillows of greys and blues and silvers. As you sit down and make yourself comfortable more women in silver robes appear. One hands you a delicious drink in a silver chalice. Another drapes you in beautiful soft fabric covered in sparkling stars. They are preparing you to meet the goddesses. You feel excited, and a little trepidatious. But soon enough, after you have had a few sips of your delicious drink and have laid back upon the comfortable cushions, you feel at peace, content in this beautiful space.

From this place of calm and rest, you look up and all of a sudden the goddesses are here. First to sit beside you is the Celtic goddess, Arianrhod.[*] Her name means the silver wheel. And as she spins her silver wheel, she weaves the fates of humans. She weaves the threads of days and nights. It reminds you that you also have this power to weave and create your days exactly as you wish them to be. Next, the Greek goddess Selene[†] appears. The Titan goddess is huge and gorgeous, a giant presence of joy. She glows with moonlight. Selene possesses a glowing chariot powered by beautiful white horses. And each night she pulls the moon across the night sky. It is said that Selene is so powerful, she can pierce illusion and connect us to our intuition. Awakening the abilities we already possess, but sometimes need reconnecting to, Selene

---

[*]   Pronounced *Ah-ry-AHN-drod*. As this is Welsh, the r sound is rolled and the final d is soft, almost "ts".

[†]   Pronounced *Se-LEEN* (UK and US) or *Se-LEEN-ee* (original Greek pronunciation)

reminds us to use our intuition: it is our innate power and connection to our own inner goddess. And our third beautiful goddess tonight – as goddesses so often like to travel in threes – is another Greek goddess. This time it is Artemis,[*] the goddess of the wilderness, wild animals and the moon. Artemis loves to be free to run through the woodland with her animal friends. She is tied to no one. She answers to no one. She reminds you, as you make your own path and claim your intentions, as you plant your seeds of dreams:

You have the power to embrace your own heart, your own dreams and your own passions. Let no one else lead you. Your path is your own.

As these three beautiful goddesses sit beside you, you feel supported by their presence, comforted and emboldened by their power. They all laugh gently together. *It is always like this,* they say. *The power is within you, all we have to do is remind you.*

You sit joyfully in this place, maybe wild Artemis rises to dance with the music. And Selene embraces you in a hug, maybe Arianrhod weaves a little silver bracelet of thread around your wrist. You spend time in this joyful place enjoying each others' company.

Pause

And although it seems the time comes so soon, it is time to leave this beautiful temple

---

of the goddesses and of the moon. The goddesses smile and wish you well on your onward journey as you travel with the cycles of the moon. They remind you that the power is always within you, and they will help watch over you as you journey through your cycles and phases.

So, as we begin to unravel from our meditation, we'll stretch a little and flicker the eyes open when you are ready. Welcome back, beautiful one.

The Library

Today's journey is to a library: a sacred space of shared knowledge, wisdom, history and story. A place many of us may find soothing to be!

Find yourself a comfortable place. As we gently close the eyes and allow the breath to become slow and peaceful. We'll take a little time to settle and to breathe. As we feel our body relaxing, we feel safe.

Pause

Allow your mind's eye to visualise yourself walking along a busy street. You're aware of the sounds of traffic and of people talking. You can see people rushing from place to place and talking on their phones. But as you continue down this busy street, something catches your eye. There is a large wooden doorway, to your left. And as you look upon it, you pause, allowing the people to continue walking around you.

You slip out of the stream of walking traffic and gently

push upon the door. It moves easily and you feel drawn to move inside, unnoticed by the people around you. You slip through the doorway and close it behind you. At once, this great heavy wooden door has muffled the sounds of the street outside. Everything feels much quieter and much stiller in this place. There is a corridor before you, and it is lit with candles: a beautiful, low, flickering light. You can smell incense in the air. This place feels peaceful: it is a sacred place. You feel drawn to walk down the corridor, unsure of where it will lead but feeling safe in your journey.

As you reach the end of the corridor, another door stands before you. Once again, it is a tall wooden door. You may notice that the wood is carved with patterns and symbols. They may mean something to you, or you may simply see them as beautiful decoration. Once again, you are drawn to push open the wooden door. And here before you, through this door, is a beautiful round room.

Upon the walls of this beautiful room, are row after row after row…of books. Bound with beautiful colours, gilded edges and words that glint in the candlelight. You feel a sense of awe in this place. All these books, all this knowledge. You take in your surroundings.

Pause

There is soft carpet beneath your feet. Candles fill the room with gentle light. This place feels truly special. As you approach a bookcase near you, perhaps you run your finger along the back of a few of the beautiful books. And as you do so, you notice each of the books have names of people along their spines. Soon enough, you see your name. A beautiful, huge, bound book has your name on the spine in glinting gold.

You gently pull it out from the bookshelf. You feel the weight of this book in your hands. You take it over to a large wooden desk and set the book down. There is a large, beautiful ribbon holding a bookmark, and as the pages fall open you see before you, in elaborate detail, all of your accumulated knowledge. It starts with your studies, your experience, the things you've seen and done. And then it moves backwards in time. The things you have learned from your mother, your grandmother, perhaps: recipes, secrets, ideas passed down through your friends and family. Further still, the details roll back to your ancestors. Their knowledge of the Earth and seasons and lunar cycles. Your wisdom extends back through many eras, many centuries, culminating in you. Take a moment to take in the details of this book. Maybe you see them as words or images or even moving pictures.

Pause

And when you feel you have taken in this sight, taken in this awareness of all the knowledge you possess, gently close this beautiful book. As you do, you notice in small letters, inscribed underneath your name, there is a little message from one of the names within this book, it might be your own name, or any of your family or ancestors – it is a reminder that you have valuable and glorious knowledge, and by sharing it with others, you can be a guide. As a priestess, as a teacher, as an inspiration. It does not matter the form in which you teach others. No matter how many lives you touch, whether it be one or one million. You are an inspiration. You have within you the wisdom of your ancestors.

Pause

So as the time comes for us to leave, just for now, our beautiful library, our book of wisdom, you place the book back upon the shelf and return along the corridor. And once more, we will walk through the wooden doorway onto the street. It's still noisy, and there are still people rushing around, but you now feel a little stronger, a little more confident as you have been reminded of your inner knowledge, your inner wisdom, your own inner guides.

As we prepare ourselves to leave our meditation, take as long as you wish to stretch, to move, to unravel. You may wish simply to sit with this meditation and allow your mind to wander and reflect on what you've seen or what you felt.

Journaling Ideas

If you wish to, take up your pen and take a little time to reflect on your knowledge. There is so much within you, this list could be very long. So, take your time. Think about all the many elements of knowledge you have, whether it be how to cook a beautiful meal, how to properly clean clothes, how to find your way on a map. And then through to academic achievements, you may reflect on the things you've learned at school, college, university… All the things passed down to you through relatives and friends: little snippets of wisdom and learning. And you can reflect on this as a reminder of how much knowledge you truly have. How much authority you have to speak as a guide of your own inner wisdom.

If you want to, you can also reflect on how you might share this knowledge. You might want to write a blog or an article for a magazine. You may look for opportunities to teach others in workshops or classes. You may even wish to begin thinking about writing a book. They are all within your grasp. You can share your knowledge in any way that you wish. Remember the importance of sharing this knowledge. Feel how you have benefited from the knowledge of others and celebrate the fact that you can now pass on yours.

Nemetona and the Sacred Grove

Join me to meet the ancient Celtic goddess Nemetona,[*] Lady of Sanctuary. Her name is drawn from the Celtic root word nemeto, *referring to spiritual space and sacred groves. She is both the embodiment and guardian goddess of this sacredness and a reminder that any place can be sacred. In this simple meditation, the goddess and I invite you to simply be, for a short time, in stillness, quiet and calm. This is our sanctuary, right here, within.*

Find your comfortable place. Close your eyes. And begin to let the day and the noise of the world fall away. Muscles of the body begin to relax. And breath begins to settle and calm.

Our goddess guide, Our Lady of Sanctuary, exists as the stillness of the end of a summer's day, when the earth is warm, and the birds sing at dusk. Where we feel peaceful and content. So perhaps in our mind's eye, we envisage ourselves in that place of stillness on a summer's evening. A sacred grove is a space of sacred trees, but your space can include anything you wish. Your sacred grove could be a field of wildflowers, a stone circle, ancient trees… Any space we hold dear in our hearts can be sacred to us. And the goddess Nemetona can hold space for us here, and we for her. She is the quiet and the light, she is the sense of sacredness and calm that fall over us in this space. There are no rules here. No right or wrong of practice and ritual. What we offer here is simply our breath and our being, and the calm within. Finding the space of

---

[*]   Pronounced *Nem-uh-TONE-uh*

sanctuary, the space of the sacred, the space in between our breaths. Each inhale and exhale. This is where the sacred space truly resides, the space of the in-between.

With the earth beneath us, the air around us, here, we simply bask: in light, in warmth, in the nature we see around us, whether that be grass, stone, rock, tree, water or wildflower.

The ancient goddess watches over us, she who has gone by many names. And like many of our oldest goddesses, she exists only in wisps and shadows, the briefest of stories. But that is okay. Because to connect to a goddess and their energy, is something we can all do. No matter how sparse the written records may be. After all, the goddesses and the great deities represent more than just names, texts or carvings. They are hope, they are feeling, they are ideas. They were created by us, as humans, to represent energies and powers we could not fathom. So when we connect to any deity, to any energy, we accept that this is a world beyond words. This is a world of the other. Of mystery and magic.

Pause

Brave ones, dear ones, as our short time in sanctuary comes to a close just for now, I invite you: next time you find yourself somewhere special to you, whether that be in the shade of a beautiful tree or resting in your own garden, take time to savour. To sit in the sacred. And the sacredness and magic of the deities around us. We may find our sacred groves in any place we come to in mindfulness and meditation.

Take your time, take some deeper breaths. Perhaps stretch out through the body. And whenever you feel ready, you can gently open your eyes. I welcome you back!

The Kitchen Witch and the Hearth Fire

Today we travel to the warmth of the hearth fire and the magical realm of the Kitchen Witch. To peek inside the kitchen of the witch is to glimpse into magic and into our past. This is a little journey to embrace the absolute joy to be found in the magic of hearth and home. Remembering the tinctures and balms of our ancestors. The jewel-bright spices, shining fruits and emerald herbs. There is magic woven so intrinsically into the threads of drawing people home, feeding them, and the laughter and healing to be found around the dining table. There's nothing quite like it. (You can read more of this magic in my books Kitchen Witch *and* The Kitchen Witch Companion*!)*

Take your time to settle into your place of relaxation, taking a pause from the day. Letting the body and the mind settle.

You may already have found your mind wandering…to the kitchen. It might be your own kitchen, the kitchen from your family home. Or a kitchen where you have felt safe and warm and nourished. Maybe even a beautiful kitchen from imagination or a story. The room is aglow with light: candles, burning lanterns…and a hearth fire crackling in the centre of the room. The beautiful scent of wood smoke in the air.

A smiling figure, a friend, stands before a bubbling cauldron. Whirls of steam rise and dance. The potion within is one to heal and soothe…

Above the flames of the hearth, in the cauldron, story, history and memory blend together, brought back to life in a sparkling moment. These create bubbles! And as these bubbles rise, they float around the room, and you see images within them. It might be a memory of meals shared with family. A romantic meal by candlelight, or one surrounded by laughter and friends. The cauldron is bubbling away, and more and more bubbles rise and float into the air. More and more memories dance in the light of the hearth fire. Allow yourself to see the bubbles. See the memories. See the joy that dances through this kitchen, and the magic you can sense here.

Pause

The dancing bubbles settle. You are handed a bowl of the most delicious food by the figure at the cauldron. Take the bowl, it is warm and smells delicious. You and your friend at the cauldron sit side by side now, by the hearth fire, in companionable silence. The memories have nourished you. The food nourishes you now. The scent and the sights and the tastes of memory.

Pause

As the time comes to leave this kitchen, know that your heart – the hearth within you – keeps these memories and joys safe. They are there waiting for whenever you need a little nourishment from memories that are sweet and magical and very precious.

So, we bid our friend farewell and leave the kitchen for now. Take some deep breaths and stretch. When you feel ready, gently open the eyes. Welcome back!

Journal Ideas

If you wish, write down any happy memories, any moments, any ideas that you recall from the journey in the kitchen. Maybe it has reminded you of an old family recipe you would like to try. Or an old memory that you would like to sit with for a little while.

The Cauldron

There is another cauldron in this meditation, and perhaps another kitchen witch. We'll journey today with the Celtic Goddess Cerridwen,[*] *a wise crone goddess, she whose cauldron represents prophecy, the spirals of life and death, transformation, and elements of magic.*

So, with transformation afoot, let's take our time to settle and relax into our chosen place for meditation. Make sure that you are warm and comfortable, and close your eyes.

We will envisage passing through a doorway that leads to a secret path deep into the earth, it might be a tunnel of rock; or of brambles and tree branches. And as you enter this passage, it is warm and well lit. There are candles burning, little lanterns flickering, casting warm light around. As you journey, you sense that you are moving downwards, a little deeper into the earth. Journeying down, down, down. Feeling relaxed and peaceful in this quiet place.

And soon, a great space opens up around you. You find yourself in an otherworldly realm. A space that feels filled with magic and knowledge, it is lined with shelves, filled with jars of herbs, berries and spices, and books in every colour.

You are met by the goddess, Cerridwen. She is as old and wise as the earth itself. You sense her serene power. She smiles at you warmly, as she takes your hand and leads you to her cauldron. This huge cast-iron cauldron sits in the centre of the room, and

* Pronounced *KE-rid-wen* (UK/US) *Ke-ri-WEN* (original Welsh pronunciation, with a rising inflection on the last syllable).

she stirs it with a great staff. The liquid inside is so beautiful. It whirls in colours and sparkles, its own swirling galaxy.

Cerridwen invites you to cast into the cauldron whatever you wish to let go of, or that you wish to be transformed. You may cast in a memory or worries, people or places. They might fall into the cauldron in the form of images or words or feelings. Take your time.

Pause

Cerridwen stirs the cauldron, she stirs, and she stirs...stirring through time and season, through magic and memory, through wisdom and hope, through endings and beginnings. Finally, she stops and reaches deep into the cauldron. She takes out what you had cast in and places it before you. Only, it is not the same: it has been transformed. Transformed into exactly what it needs to be. The item or items you have cast in may look different, you may feel differently about them. Or maybe they have transformed by disappearing completely.

Cerridwen, as the goddess of transformation, reminds us that we can always let go of what does not serve us. She reminds us that life moves in cycles and spirals, death and rebirth. In letting go of some things, new things can be reborn. This circular dance mirrored in the spirals of the cauldron and the cycles of the year is an invitation, an opportunity, always, to transform.

Pause

The time has come to thank Cerridwen for what she has shown you today. She smiles at you warmly and bids you farewell. You take with you what has been transformed in the cauldron as you journey mindfully, back the way you came. Rising, rising, rising…until you reach once more the entrance, and step into the light of the day .

Take a deep breath, and return to your place here in your day, here in this room. And when you feel ready, you may open your eyes and return to your day.

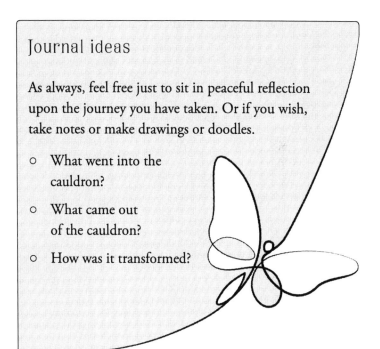

Journal ideas

As always, feel free just to sit in peaceful reflection upon the journey you have taken. Or if you wish, take notes or make drawings or doodles.

- o What went into the cauldron?

- o What came out of the cauldron?

- o How was it transformed?

End of Section Two - Notes for Reflection

○ Which archetypes, deities or spirit spoke to you? You may wish to journey with them again or learn more about their stories in history and myth, and the culture from which they came.

○ Perhaps you found some challenging. Take time to reflect on this too – perhaps the Queen archetype made you feel uncomfortable because you are not used to standing in your power, or maybe it was embracing the archetype of the Crone. Feel free to reflect and explore without judgement.

○ This section explores some places and spaces that could be considered sacred. Make a note of places that mean something to you, be that a stone circle, hometown, a beach, or forest. Can you visit these places to meditate within them? Or create your own meditation taking time to visualise your own sacred space?

○ Is there anywhere in your own body – another kind of sacred space – that you feel you could send extra healing or love to? What healing words might you send, for example, to your heart? Make notes in your journal if you wish. You may use these notes for reflection or use them to create your own mantras.

JOURNEYING WITH THE ELEMENTS

Working with the elements can help us find balance and harmony. In the practice of sympathetic magic, 'like affects like'. Need a little spark for your day? Meditate with fire. Whereas if you feel that you have too much fire energy dominant – feeling excessive anger, overwhelm or an inability to settle – you may wish to find elements of water or earth in meditation. Feeling stuck? Try meditating with freedom of air or flowing water. Take some time to make a note of the element that speaks to you today and reflect on what this may mean: are you trying to bring more of this element into your life? Or gently bring an overabundance into balance?

Create your own list of what you associate with each element – can you bring the element with you to your meditations or your space? For example, lighting a candle for fire, or incense for air, placing a stone nearby for earth or a small dish of liquid or seashell for water.

The Four Elements

In this meditation series we delve into the power of the elements, the very building blocks of the Earth and universe. Each meditation in this little series will start the same way: offering the chance to relax and unwind before we visit our element.

We can observe the four Western elements – earth, air, fire and water – and their correspondences in our own lives. Connecting with them helps us to find harmony with the elemental energy of the season and of our own nature.

Element of Earth

Welcome to the element of earth. In this practice, we'll connect to the earth on a very special journey through the sun and rain. Connect with the ground beneath your feet, feel the soil and take a long deep breath to smell the air.

Take this opportunity to make yourself comfortable. When you feel relaxed in your body, you can gently close the eyes. Allowing the attention to settle. Allowing yourself the time and space with each breath to fill the lungs on the inhale and empty them on the exhale, connecting to that unhurried rhythm. We'll let go of thoughts of work schedules, deadlines, let go of the busyness of the day. For a short while, we can press pause on the world and spend some time within. Taking our time to settle and relax.

Pause

Now from this place of calm and restfulness, we will bring to the mind's eye the element of earth: the great Earth Mother beneath us; the ground, dirt, grit and bone beneath our feet. To journey towards the magic of this earth element we will imagine standing in a great field with green grass beneath our feet. We are barefoot and the grass is soft and cool underneath our feet and between our toes. A great fiery sun shines above us amidst the blue sky. We feel warm and calm in this place of nature. This place of green and blue and fiery yellow.

We begin to walk peacefully along the grass, enjoying the calm space. We might hear a bird chirping in a distant tree. Maybe the sound of longer grass whispering in the wind. But it is a very peaceful place, a very quiet place within which we wander. As we continue to walk in no particular direction, we find that the grass begins to dissipate, and our feet now feel soft, red earth. It is a warm day, so the earth is very dry underneath your feet. It feels warm and powdery. Maybe you pick up a small handful and let it crumble between your fingers. You smell the earthy scent of the soil and it is comforting to you.

The blue sky above you begins to fill with grey clouds, becoming overcast, and in just a moment, it begins to rain. Great round large raindrops begin splashing around you. They feel cool upon your skin. And those big raindrops bounce upon the dry earth, throwing up dust and a beautiful scent of summer days. A scent known as *petrichor*.* It is the smell of dry earth and dust and water mixing on a hot day. It might bring back memories of camping or playing in the street as a child and getting caught in a downpour. It is a beautiful scent and you stand in the rain letting the cool water drop upon your skin.

The downpour is heavy but brief, and before long the rain has stopped. You feel refreshed. And you see that the earth beneath you has absorbed the water and become much darker and thicker, like a clay or paste. You have so enjoyed the coolness of the water that you pick up a great handful of this newly soft wet earth. It feels cool between your fingers. And just a little bit gritty and grainy. And what do you do with this great handful of earth? You can't resist! You smear it over your arms and up onto your shoulders. You take another handful and cover your chest and tummy. You sweep the mud over your legs, over your neck and onto your face like a facemask.

You are covered in this beautiful cooling earth. It feels soothing and nourishing. And you can smell that lovely, earthy scent on your skin. It feels fun to play in the mud and cover your skin with it. So just for a little while, lie down on the ground. Once again, a blue sky is above us, and the bright sun is shining down. The earth slowly dries out on our skin, gently lightening and cracking. It feels so warm and soothing, as if this earth is drawing out any toxins, any negativity, any stress. It's drawing it out through our skin. It feels like a really

---

* Pronounced *PEH-truh-cor*.

cleansing process. The earth is drawing out anything that we don't need.

When the earth upon our skin has completely dried we stand up. The cracked dry earth falls cleanly from our body in chunks and crumbles and, all at once, the earth that was upon our skin has fallen back to the ground. But the beautiful earth has left its mark upon our skin. Great swirling patterns like henna tattoos swirl over our bodies. Beautiful shapes of nature appear on our skin: spirals, images of trees and birds, oceans and clouds. All the beautiful images of the earth are etched upon our skin. Reminding us that we are all connected. We leave our mark upon the earth and the earth leaves its mark upon us.

You feel very connected to the earth as you take your next steps into the natural world. And we once more find that green grass beneath our feet as we retrace our steps back to our starting place. The great glow of the sun above us shines strong. And we see the markings upon our skin begin to fade and disappear. But this special journey, this special moment of connection with the earth has left its mark within, as we remember the great gifts and abundance of the earth, the soil, the grit, the dirt. It gifts us so much every single day from the food we eat, to the elements that build our houses, homes and cars. The earth gives us everything we need.

And so, my darlings, when you feel ready to leave this meditation, take a few deep breaths. Take your time to arrive back in the room as we return to the day.

Element of Air

Air surrounds us, touching our skin in this very moment. It is the wind that moves the clouds, the breezes that we see and hear moving branches and grasses. In today's practice, we will journey on the breeze and take flight with the element of air (and just a little help from a goddess!)

Take this opportunity to make yourself comfortable. When you feel relaxed in your body, you can gently close the eyes. Allowing the attention to settle. Allowing yourself the time and space with each breath to fill the lungs on the inhale and empty them on the exhale, connecting to that unhurried rhythm. We'll let go of thoughts of work schedules, deadlines, let go of the busyness of the day. For a short while, we can press pause on the world and spend some time within. Taking our time to settle and relax.

Pause

Now from this place of calm and restfulness we will bring to the mind's eye the element of air. The beautiful element of air can lift us up, helping us to rise and fly like birds on the wind. Air can help inspire our imagination. And today, when we think of this element of air, a goddess is going to join us to help us on our journey.

Today, we will channel and connect to the archetype of the great Greek goddess Nike,[*] the goddess of victory. She is often

---

[*] Pronounced *NAI-kee.*

portrayed with great, beautiful wings that help her rise and fly. And with her help, we will envisage here, in this restful place, in our mind's eye, that we too have great wings. And these wings are made up of feathers that represent to us the things that help us rise.

○ Some feathers may represent family and friends.

○ Some may represent the things that excite us: new projects, adventures, travel, reading, food…

○ Some, the things that nourish us: books, learning, sharing time with friends, spending time in nature…

Allow yourself time here to envisage all the things that create your wings – friends, family, joy and love – that create a great, beautiful patchwork of coloured feathers.

Pause

With these beautiful wings you find have the strength to fly. Perhaps you envisage yourself gently rising, floating on warm air like a seabird or taking a few great strong movements with your wings like a swan rising from a lake.

Rise up, dear one! Rise into the air and fly with the strength of your wings. The ground beneath you seems smaller now. So perhaps you fly over places you know: houses and buildings, beaches and hills. Let your wings carry you. They are made up of all the things that make you strong and that make you, *you*. Here, up in the air, the world is quiet. We are far from noise, distraction, and busy thoughts here, as we fly over this great, beautiful Earth beneath us. We are at one with our own elements, our own strength, and power. Take your time to fly, dear one. Fly wherever you wish. You have this power.

Pause

When the time comes, when you feel ready, you can use your beautiful wings to gently sail on the breeze down towards the Earth, floating unhurriedly as you gently descend.

Your feet once again touch the earth. You feel joyful and connected to the elements and your own power here. And as we reconnect to the earth, we find that our wings gently disappear. But even though we cannot see them, just like the air, we trust and we know that they are always there.

So as the time comes to leave this meditation today, feel free to take some nice deep breaths. Whenever you feel ready, you can gently open the eyes. I wish you a beautiful rest of your day.

Element of Fire

This meditation will focus on the power of the element of fire, from warming embers to dancing flames.

Take this opportunity to make yourself comfortable. When you feel relaxed in your body, we can gently close the eyes. Allowing the attention to settle. Allowing yourself the time and space with each breath to fill the lungs on the inhale and empty them on the exhale, connecting to that unhurried rhythm. We'll let go of thoughts of work schedules, deadlines, let go of the busyness of the day. For a short while, we can press pause on the world and spend some time within. Taking our time to settle and relax.

Pause

We will bring to the mind's eye the element of fire.

Allow yourself to visualise fire in front of you. It may be a crackling open fire providing warmth and light, the flames dancing over logs. It might be gentle burning embers. It might be a candle flame flickering before you. Allow yourself to bring the flames and fire to mind. Fire is the element of light, of energy, but most importantly, the element of transformation.

That which we cast into the fire can be changed, transformed. So, as we visualise these flames, these embers, this flickering fire before us, think about what may serve you to throw into the fire, into the flames, to let go of. You may envisage within the flickering flames images of that which you wish to release. You may cast away old grudges, old hurts. You may envisage yourself writing events or stories or images on

119

pieces of paper and then casting them into the flames. Allow yourself this time to cast into the flames anything you wish to let go of that no longer serves you.

Pause

These things we cast into the flames, if we envisage them on pieces of paper, we may see them crumble and dissolve in the flames. The images may curl into smoke and drift away on the breeze. Allow the fire to transform, to take away these things that weigh you down or hold you back.

Pause

When you feel ready to do so, when you feel that you have cast all you wish into the flames, it is time for us to transform ourselves.

We may imagine that we step into the fire, into the embers. Or perhaps the flickering flames of the candles rise tall and surround us in spirals and curls. We are all at once surrounded by warmth and light, but we feel safe; the flames that whirl around us simply warm upon our skin. We are protected here. And as we feel this light and warmth whirl around us, we are transforming. We are letting go. We are finding strength. We are changing.

Allow yourself time to bathe in the transformative power of these flames.

Pause

As the time comes to step out of the fire, out of the flames, we feel energised and reborn as we continue our journey, finding new strength, new ways to transform as we grow and change. And any time we become aware of things that we wish to let go of, that may hold us back, there is always the chance to cast them into the fire, and bring ourselves back to our own inner power, our own inner fire and our own inner strength.

When the time comes to leave the meditation, take your time as you gently move and bring awareness back to the body. And just when you feel ready to do so, you can gently open your eyes.

Element of Water

This meditation will focus on the power of the element of water. Water is the element of flow, rhythm and connection. Associated with dreams and the realm of emotions, the water element purifies, clarifies and connects.

Take this opportunity to make yourself comfortable. When you feel relaxed in your body, you can gently close the eyes. Allowing the attention to settle. Allowing yourself the time and space with each breath to fill the lungs on the inhale and empty them on the exhale, connecting to that unhurried rhythm. We'll let go of thoughts of work schedules, deadlines, let go of the busyness of the day. For a short while, we can press pause on the world and spend some time within. Taking our time to settle and relax.

Pause

We will bring to the mind's eye the element of water. Water is an element that represents finding our rhythm in the world, finding our own pace in our own way. Just like the gentle ebb and flow of the waves upon the shore, there is power within that rhythm, but it is unhurried. No one can rush the waves.

So, as we prepare to take our journey exploring the element of water, I want you to imagine standing barefoot in front of a beautiful body of water. It might be a vast, shining ocean sparkling under the sun. It might be a great pool, rippling with gentle winds. You may find yourself standing in front of a babbling brook, river, or stream. Allow yourself to bring the image of the water in front of you to mind. Maybe in this place, you hear the sound of the water as it trickles or sparkles or splashes around you. Maybe you smell the salty ocean air or the fresh scent of a glacial stream. Perhaps you find yourself standing in front of a great waterfall and you feel the splashes of droplets on your face. Or the sea spray that whips and whirls in the wind. Take your time to use all of your senses to embody this place beside the water.

Feeling completely safe and comfortable beside this water source, we will take a few gentle steps toward it, to sink our toes and feet into the water. Perhaps you notice the gentle ripples of the water around your ankles. Feel the water washing over your feet. Is the water cooling and cleansing or is it warm and welcoming? Let the water bubble and froth around you. With your feet now in the water, you feel a connection to this liquid, this element. It moves and flows in its own way, just as we can connect to our own rhythms and our own ebbs and flows. As the water moves, we are reminded of the liquid in our own veins, which carries all we need for life around our bodies. Enjoying this sense of connection, we move deeper into the water, feeling safe and calm to do so. You may find yourself up to your waist now in this water. Feeling the liquid around you. Feeling the buoyancy and support of this water flowing and whirling around you.

You feel safe to move a little deeper into the water. It may be that now you allow your whole body to be immersed in the water. If you are in front of a waterfall, perhaps you step underneath the deluge and allow yourself to be washed completely in the cascading waters. If you imagined that you are standing before a stream or babbling brook, maybe you lie down on some smooth stones and allow the water to swirl around you.

In whatever way that feels right for you and the images in your mind, allow yourself to be surrounded by this element of water. Let the water wash over you, let it surround you. Let it support you. Allow it to wash away anything you wish to let go of. The water can help support us in that which we want to pursue and hold on to, but it can also wash away the things we don't want to hold onto. Allow this wonderful element to support you exactly as you need.

Pause

As the time comes to leave our sanctuary of water, of waves and ripples, we'll gently rise from the water, feeling our feet on solid earth. Perhaps you envisage wrapping yourself in something warm and cosy.

Begin, once more, to be aware of your surroundings here in this soft and restful place. And even though we are now bringing our awareness back to the room, you feel refreshed and revived from our time with the water element, renewed from our time in the water, perhaps a little lighter from that which you have allowed to be washed away.

So, when you feel ready to do so, gently open the eyes and stretch if you want to, as we return to the world.

Elemental Inspirations

We'll bring our elemental journey, and the journey of this book, to a close with meditations with the Earth Mother, a sun goddess, and deities of ice, ocean and root. If you feel inspired to do so gather other stories, myths or archetypes of deities that may help you connect to an element. I have already mentioned some in this section, here are a few more examples of goddesses that are connected to certain elements:

○ *Water: Aphrodite (Greek)*

○ *Earth: Gaia, Demeter (Greek)*

○ *Air: Dogoda (Slavic), Tuuletar, (Finnish)*

○ *Fire: Vesta (Roman), Hestia (Greek)*

Sunshine, Fire and the Goddess Sekhmet

In this practice, we'll journey with the beautiful Egyptian goddess Sekhmet.* Who, as well as being a beautiful solar goddess, is a goddess of fire and healing. You may enjoy creating a little solar flame of your own and lighting a candle for this meditation. If that's not convenient, then feel free just to envisage a candle flame in your mind's eye. If you do light a candle, be sure to place it somewhere safe. You might want to be seated so you can gaze upon the candle, or you might be happy to lie down, and you might either watch the light on the walls and the ceiling, or just close your eyes and have a sense of that warmth of the flame behind your eyes.

I invite you now to find your restful place for meditation. Allow yourself to settle and relax. Enjoy a sense that the light from this small flame is surrounding you with light and warmth. A healing circle of light surrounds you. We take our time to envisage that circle surrounding us, protecting us, guiding us: a safe space of calm and peace where we can allow ourselves to relax.

We can relax and consciously release the body. We can relax the legs and feet. Relaxing the arms and elbows all the way to the tips of your fingers. Relaxed and peaceful. Letting a wave of calm radiate through the hips, tummy, heart and chest. And shining up through the neck and jaw all the way to the

---

*   Pronounced *SEK-met.*

very top of your head. We allow ourselves this time to journey towards peace. A little step or two towards calm.

Pause

Sekhmet is a powerful goddess of sun, of light and of healing. And there is a beautiful story that tells that whenever Sekhmet breathes out, she breathes fire, creating light and warmth to her homeland of Egypt. That was the breath of Sekhmet.

So, as the light and warmth of our candle glows around us gently, we are going to recreate that very simple breath of Sekhmet. Taking a nice deep inhale through the nose, then sigh and exhale through the mouth. Inhale through the nose. And exhale through the mouth.

Allowing each exhale to be a release. Breathing out a gentle fire, just like the goddess breathes into flame, into light. Letting go of that which you wish to release. But also connecting to this fire, this candle, this light. We are sending our own breath of fire out into the world. And letting it surround us, blending, mingling with that candle flame.

The light and the warmth and the flames grow stronger around us, creating a healing fire. This healing fire can take whatever form comes to your mind: it might be the healing warmth of sand underneath you, like the sand dunes of Egypt. It might be a great golden sun above you, shining upon you. It might be flickering flames or warm embers, bringing warmth, but also holding the great power to burn away. Allow yourself to be here fully, to pause, to breathe in this light. You are surrounded by this glowing light, this warmth, this energy. We create this healing light for ourselves. The power is already there within us.

As we invoke the power of light, of fire, and the energy of the goddess, perhaps Sekhmet joins you. She might come to sit beside you or watch over you. You may envisage her, perhaps in her goddess form, with the body of a woman and the head of a beautiful lioness. Or maybe you envisage her as someone who represents that energy of fire and healing. Or maybe today that energy of the goddess comes to you as simply a light, warmth, like a flame or sunbeam shining upon you, surrounding you, and holding you.

This love of the goddess that we may feel within is also connected to Sekhmet's energy of fiery strength and the flames. So, when we think of this love for ourselves, it might be in a passive form, in taking time for ourselves to rest and heal. But it also might embody that fiery strength of Sekhmet's in that we can be proactive in our self-care as well. We may consciously say no to things that are draining us or are not right for us. We may consciously and mindfully separate or burn away things that are not serving us. So do not be afraid to embody the strength of this powerful goddess to take your steps forward in claiming what you need: what you need for healing, what you need in terms of time and rest and self-love. And when connecting to your true self, your authentic self, your own path, there may be elements within that that you're not sure about yet, and that is okay as well. We can claim our journey and our next steps. Under that light of love of the goddess. She's watching over us. She's reminding us of the strength within ourselves to find our own path. Our own path to wholeness and to healing. Here the candlelight can be a symbol of our way being lit. Of light and warmth to guide our way, upon our path, upon our journey.

Pause

Let's take our time to bring our awareness back to the room and back to the day. Perhaps take some deeper breaths and stretch or move the body. Give yourself a little time to rise without hurry, without rush. Now, perhaps we may take the candle that has been burning, and bring it before us. And with just a little thanks and gratitude to the goddess for this vision of light and healing fire, gently blow out the flame, knowing that you can come back to this place, you can come back to this flame, the light of the goddess whenever you wish.

These simple rituals of connecting to the goddess within ourselves can be powerful reminders of that beautiful power of the goddess around us. She is within the candle flames, within the sunlight, within the warmth…she is wherever we need her to be. Whether we wish to connect to her via a simple ritual or within meditation, she is always there. And that can be a comfort. So for now, my darling one, I will send you thanks and blessings and love for joining me today.

Earth Mother

This meditation will help us connect to the great Earth Mother. We see the archetype of the Earth Mother figure in such deities as the Greek goddess Gaia and the Roman goddess Terra. Goddesses such as these represent the ancestral mothers of all life, the primal creators of animals, humans and plants. Not only do they represent the Earth as a planet, but the earth beneath our feet: the dirt, the compost that creates somewhere for life to grow from. Many Earth goddesses were also goddesses of childbirth, fertility and abundance, so closely linked are all these beautiful elements of nature and our dependence on nourishment from the Earth. We could not exist if it wasn't for the Earth Mother, so it is always important both to express gratitude for her and do all we can to protect her.

If there is any possibility that you can comfortably do this meditation outside on the earth, on the grass or on the sand, then please do that.

Let's start, as always, by finding a comfortable place, somewhere where you can rest comfortably. We allow the body to relax and settle as we take a little time with the Earth goddesses. And as we gently close the eyes, we begin to allow the body to surrender into the earth. It is safe to let go. The Earth goddesses are holding you within their hands. The earth is solid and strong and can support you as you allow the body to relax and the mind to come to calm.

Pause

We'll take ourselves on a little journey in our mind's eye.

With bare feet we find ourselves standing upon soft green grass, on a beautiful green hill overlooking a land of beauty. From your hilltop, you can see for miles. And you can take in every beautiful element that the Earth Mother has to offer. You can see lakes, streams and bodies of water. You can see great fields of green and fields of crops of golden wheat and maize. You can see great tall trees and maybe some blossoming fruit trees as well as flowers and shrubs. And maybe you catch a glimpse of a few of the animals that are supported by nature's bounty. Take your time to draw in this beautiful patchwork quilt of colours and elements of the natural world. You may see before you scenes from memory or imagination or whatever comes to your mind right now. Take your time to take it in. Allow yourself to visualise this place fully.

Pause

Feeling grounded and calm from your hilltop, you feel drawn to descend just a little. You notice as you drop down the slope that there is an entrance that runs underneath the hill and you are drawn to move away from the beautiful light and warmth around you and into the dark shadows of this entrance.

Even though it is dark, it is also warm and peaceful. And as you enter into the space, you smell the beautiful scent of soil and earth and stone: this place feels very ancient, very safe. You feel your bare feet move from soft grass to warm, soft earth. You feel your feet and toes gently sink into the mud. And, as you walk into the place below the hill, you see there are steps descending deep into the heart of the hill, deep into the heart of the land and deep into the heart of the Earth.

You follow a passageway. The space gets darker. But also warmer. As you move into this space under the hill, the sounds and light of the outside world become muffled and fade. You are brought into a space of complete quiet. The corridor you're walking down widens. And you come to the centre of this space under the hill. There is light streaming down from above. As you gaze upwards, you see the roots of trees casting patterns through the earth, like amazing stained glass windows made of roots. They cast a gentle light into this space. The earthen floor is warm and helps you feel rooted, so safe under the earth, in the earth, of the Earth: warm and sheltered.

In this most simple of temples to the Earth Goddess, you take your seat upon the earth. Take a few quiet minutes, just being with the Earth, being with the goddess, being with the rhythm of your breath and your heart. Being in silence.

Pause

Having spent a few quiet minutes bathing in the silence and the warmth of the Earth, whenever you feel ready to rise, begin walking away from this sacred space and once again enter back into the world of green grass and blue skies and trees and plants, all the more grateful for both the light and the dark that the Earth offers us, and the abundance of beauty.

When you feel ready to do so, take some nice deep breaths. Gently open the eyes and come back to the world.

The Goddesses of Ice

This meditation started with a request from a gorgeous soul who was seeking a meditation of ice as an element of expansion and protection. I was instantly inspired by the image of the ice goddesses and giantesses of Norse and Celtic folklore. Huge, powerful women of shattering power: makers, breakers, creators of mountains and islands, unafraid to take up space in the world. So, I offer you this story of ice, goddesses and powerful space. The ice maidens cometh…

Greetings, dear ones, and welcome to a meditation and story journey today where we will work with the element of ice. Ice can be an inspiration if we choose to see it as such, just as the elements of water, air, fire and earth. Ice is strong, it expands, it takes up space. Ice can be destructive, but also preservative, and it can create great beauty. Ice holds things solidly. Ice connects to many a beautiful wintery goddess. And so, they will also join us on this journey.

We may be thinking of ice, but we want to be nice and warm and cosy and restful. So, take your time to wrap yourself in blankets, support yourself with cushions. Allow yourself to feel comfortable. Allowing body, mind and breath to settle in their own way and in your own time. Here, perhaps we are still with the element of water as we just allow any tensions or tightness to flow, to trickle away from the body. Flowing away from us like a babbling brook or a trickling stream. Feel the tensions of the day wash away like a sudden downpour of rain, which falls upon us and washes away the day. In our mind's eye, we can cross over a threshold and let go of the noise of the day, and move into our inner world.

Pause

We find ourselves in a land of frost and ice. We are in a place of nature. We see blades of grass trimmed with little sparkling white edges of frost. There is a gentle crunch beneath our feet as we walk. Perhaps there are drifts of snow. We journey along this frosty grass path, etched with shimmering ice trimmings on each branch, each leaf, each plant. The world is quiet and glittering here. On your path, you see ahead of you a beautiful frozen lake. The ice of this lake is thick and strong. And you feel safe as you step upon its smooth surface. Solid ice beneath your feet. Walking out a little further towards the centre of this lake, you see beautiful seams of bubbles and re-frozen cracks within the ice. Encapsulated within this frozen water, you might also see leaves, twigs, berries… Little jewels of nature frozen in time creating this beautiful, strong surface. Each crack is visible, but then refrozen. Each little item adding to the richness of this beautiful structure: these are not impurities, they are enrichments.

Standing tall and standing strong on this beautiful, icy surface, you feel empowered. You have a sense of this space around you, a sense of the ice beneath you. Standing tall and standing strong. A sense of expansion, just as water expands to create ice. You expand, stand in your strength.

You become aware that around the edges of the lake, the trees and the plants form a circle of support around you. And perhaps within those icy sparkles, within the edge of the lake, there is also a sense that surrounding you are the great and powerful goddesses of winter, of snow, of ice. The great crone goddess, the Cailleach,[*] with beautiful white hair and white clothes. She who moves mountains. Who creates islands out of rocks. So strong, so powerful, she can move the Earth through its seasons. The Norse goddesses, Skadi,[†] the huntress, who enjoys being out in the snow. She moves through snow and ice with such strength and joy. And also, Norse goddesses Freya and Frigg; goddesses of love and magic, at home in the magical northern lights and long, dark winter nights. And alongside these goddesses, there are the great giantesses of Norse mythology; movers of mountains. There is even a story of two giantesses that took a giant stone salt mill and made so much salt that they filled the oceans with it. They were strong and big enough to create all the salt within all the oceans. And when I think of these goddesses, these giants, they embody ice beautifully, because they are great and

---

[*]   Cailleach can be pronounced *KAY-lackh* or *KAI-lyackh* in Irish and Scots Gaelic dependant on regional accent.

[†]   Pronounced *SKA-di* (UK/US), *SKAH-tdi* (traditional Norse).

powerful women who take up space in the world. They are just as big, as huge, as they need to be in presence, and in energy. *Do not be afraid to take up space in this world.* That is what the goddesses of ice tell us.

Perhaps you envisage these beautiful goddesses standing around you. Maybe you simply see them within the ice, in the glistening frosts or the swathes of snow around you. They are always there, whether we see them or not. They stand tall with us. They stand strong with us. They make. They break. They create. They take up as much space as they need. Expanding into power. Into divine feminine energy.

Pause

As our time upon the ice with our beautiful goddesses draws to a close, as always, there is no rush. You may stay as long as you wish with the elements, with the ice, with the frost, with the goddesses.

If you are ready, we will draw back along the frosted path. It may be that we arrive somewhere cosy and warm. Maybe there are blankets and hot drinks waiting for us, merriment and love. Perhaps we are home or somewhere special to us. (Or maybe the Norse goddesses invite you into their feasting halls!)

Wherever we end up, there is an element of our journey with the ice that we carry onwards with us, a knowing that there is a strength within the ice that we can always connect to, whatever the season, wherever we are. A remembering that we have power to flow as water or to stand strong as ice. To slow down, and to expand into our space. Breathe deep. And stand tall.

As I leave you now, my ice queens, my frost giants, my ice goddesses, I wish you a beautiful day.

The Ocean and Morgan le Fay

Morgan le Fay has many embodiments and is found in many myths and stories and songs. We may recognize her name from Arthurian legend, but Morgan herself is far more ancient, and has many more tales to her name than simply this side-story alongside King Arthur. She was known to be a mermaid, sorceress, fairy, and siren. But, as is so often the way with powerful women, she has been portrayed in negative ways. This inspired me to create this story journey: a meditation for days when maybe we feel misunderstood or misrepresented. Morgan, with her many tales, her many embodiments, her many strands of magic can offer us inspiration and guidance.

Find a place that feels comfortable and restful for you. A place where you feel warm and supported. As we connect to the rise and fall of the breath, let it move through the body like a gentle wave drawing in. And drawing out. Allowing the noise and busyness of the day to drift from you. Floating upon still waters away from you.

Pause

In our mind's eye, we envisage ourselves standing overlooking the ocean. And this ocean may reflect feelings you're currently experiencing in your day or in your life. If you feel calm and settled, the water may be still, reflecting the sunlight and the clouds above. If you are feeling fractious or stressed, the water may be choppy. If you are feeling anger, maybe great, crashing waves and frothing white horses thunder towards the shore. Allow yourself to witness the ocean and hear its song.

Allow yourself to take in this experience of gazing out over the ocean and seeing its waves, its cycles, its rhythms. These many faces of the ocean reflect our moods and our energy. Just as the many faces of goddess Morgan le Fay can represent the many facets of ourselves.

This is a goddess who embodies the many powers of the ocean, both powerful and beautiful. Dangerous and changeable. And you may envisage Morgan le Fay as a beautiful mermaid, or a fearsome siren, empowered, feminine, divine. She embodies every side of our being, both the beauty and abundance of the mermaid, and also, the changeable nature and the fury of the siren song, fury at the injustice of their situation.

Her name, 'Morgan' means a goddess of water. 'Le Fay' speaks to her connection with the fairy land, the fae, the fairies. A world of magic. And Morgan le Fay is also represented as a fairy queen, as a sorceress.

Morgan le Fay represents the Otherworld, the energy that lives within: sparkles and hidden glances, illusions, images out of focus, a world of the other. From a place looking out over the ocean we may imagine ourselves as Morgan le Fay. Or perhaps one of her archetypes: mermaid, siren, sorceress, fairy goddess, empowered woman. She is connected to the elements of the physical world. But also to the energetic and spiritual. To the deep, dark, silent underworld of the ocean where all is quiet. And to the light and sparkling land of magic, of fairies, of flowers. There is such power in these contradictions. We too can find power in embracing every cycle and rhythm, each element of the divine feminine and of ourselves.

Here we can dive into dark and quiet waters. Settle near

the gentle whirls of the waves. As we connect to the image of the ocean, we become aware of the songs of the sea that are different for us all. Of waves lapping or crashing to shore. Of seashells held to our ears. The cry of seagulls. We may hear the songs of mermaids or sirens. The tinkling music of sand and pebbles dancing or retreating waves.

Here, we may weave our own songs. Songs that roar like banshees. Whispered wishes. The gentle song of healing waters and sacred waves under the light of the moon. The songs and the myths and the stories. They connect us to a power, a power of the divine feminine.

The power of the ocean. The power of water. Its gentle strength and rhythm shaping the Earth, and all souls. Magical, powerful, ruthless, and wild, we are all these things and more. Like the many stories of Morgan Le Fay. We are all and we are one.

Pause

Let us once again, bring our awareness to the breath, as a rolling **wave. The gentle** power and rhythm of the **breath, drawing** us back to the room an**d back to our** day, as we journey to th**e end of this** meditation today. May **you go forth** with love and power, emb**racing every** element of your inner world: the rough seas and the calm waters, the fairy queen and the sorceress.

Tree Roots

This meditation is one I created many years ago in honour of Earth Day (22nd April) but one may well argue that every day is Earth Day!

Start by finding yourself a comfortable place to rest and relax. It might be a chair or on the ground or on your yoga mat. Make sure that you feel warm and comfortable and supported and restful. As we spend a few moments breathing slowly, deeply and calmly, beginning to quieten the mind as we move into a place of feeling relaxed and focused.

Perhaps imagine the mind as a clear blue sky on a summer's day. When we start this meditation, we might have a few thoughts and ideas whirling around in our mind. Maybe we've got a few clouds in the sky. Maybe a few birds flying around. Maybe a vapour trail or two. Then, as we allow the focus to rest on the breath, it's as though we are actively clearing the sky. The clouds are drifting away. The vapour trails are fading and the birds are flying off. As we allow the thoughts to become still and fall away, we are left with the beautiful, clear blue sky. A few new little clouds may drift through the mind during the meditation, it's no problem, we'll just gently encourage them to drift on by. Not holding onto anything too tightly.

And we'll begin to bring our attention to the very base of our spine. Imagine that with each breath the base of our spine is stretching roots down into the Earth. Feel these roots move through surfaces beneath you: paving slabs, concrete, grass… And then moving further into the rich, dark soil that blankets the planet. Feeling the coolness of the Earth as you move deeper. Moving away from air and light and noise with each breath. Allow your roots to move ever deeper through underground springs, through caves filled with crystals and stalactites. Moving through the layers of the Earth as your roots spread ever deeper towards the heart of our planet.

Your roots move deeper towards the centre of the Earth. Perhaps you begin to feel the heat coming from the Earth's core, moving towards the molten centre of the planet. And as your roots reach the very heart of the Earth, allow yourself to bask in this deep connection to the planet. Feel grounded, feel centred. Appreciate both your own body, and the body of the planet that supports you. And the connection between these two special bodies.

When you're ready, you begin to imagine drawing energy from this very centre of the Earth through your roots. With each breath, you draw up power, stability, grounding and love. You see this energy rise through your roots back up through the Earth's layers, slowly with each breath. This energy rises back through caves of crystals, water springs, the paving slabs, grass… Gently the energy rises. It slowly reaches the very base of your spine. Notice any sensations or colours that come to mind, observing and allowing them without judgement.

Begin drawing this energy into your body at the very base of your spine. You might imagine this energy as a warmth, as a glowing light, a spiralling energy, or anything that comes to mind.

○ This energy sinks into our root chakra. The centre of our connection to our body and to the Earth beneath us.

o The energy continues to rise through root chakra, to our sacral chakra, our centre of creativity.

o As we breathe up this energy further still it comes to our solar plexus chakra, our centre of personal power.

o This energy continues to rise into our heart chakra, our centre of love, compassion and kindness. Feeling love and kindness envelop you as the energy of the Earth rises up.

o Now, allow the energy to come up into your throat chakra, centre of communication, as we reflect on the power of speaking truth from our heart.

o Feel the energy rise to the third eye chakra, place of vision and intuition.

o And as this energy continues to rise, it finally reaches the very top of your head, the crown chakra.

o And we imagine in our minds, this energy bursting forth through the crown chakra out to the top of the head like branches of a tree. These branches unfurl and reach up and out towards the heavens. Up and out towards the edges of the horizon. And as we rest here, we enjoy this connection between ourselves, Earth, the sky, the universe beyond.

Pause

As the time approaches for us to draw up our roots and roll in our branches, remember that we are always connected to the Earth and the world around us. It is always useful to give ourselves time to journey into the Earth, not only in our mind's eye but in real life: to connect to nature, to the seasons, to air, to ground. So take the opportunity any time you can. To journey towards the Earth.

In your mind's eye, begin drawing up the roots you sent down into the Earth. And drawing in the branches from above you, drawing in all the energy and light you have gathered today.

Allow the next few breaths to be a little longer, a little deeper. Feel free to gently move the body in any way that feels nice for you. And just when you're ready, you can gently open your eyes. Welcome back to the room.

Thank you so much for joining me for today's meditation. I hope you take each and every opportunity to enjoy the beautiful Earth on which we live. Get outside and enjoy nature. Enjoy Mother Earth, and treat her with every kindness and respect.

Final Reflections

As we come to the end of this magical collection of meditations, I hope you have found the journey enlightening. Meditation is such a powerful and wonderful tool; I hope you find great joy in bringing it into your regular practice. Here are some final things to reflect on as I leave you here to continue your journey into meditation.

You cannot do it wrong, because there is no one 'right' way.

Your meditation practice is a time just for you. In moments of quiet, we let go of the busy lives we lead and draw our attention inwards. We all have to start somewhere. If that is just a few moments of calm in the quiet of morning, or shutting out the world and feeling completely relaxed in a hot bath, then congratulations, you are meditating. There are a multitude of approaches, theories, and philosophies of meditation and mindfulness. These can seem overwhelming. But we can all make a start by simply sitting down and taking some breaths. Your body, breath and mind are your finest tools, and all that are needed to practice... You can explore different types of meditation if you wish: all are valid, and all can be effective. All can be part of your journey toward a meditation practice: this internal work is personal to you.

It can be useful to remember that when you sit down to meditate, your mind will wander. This is an inevitable truth for beginners and more seasoned meditators alike. The art of meditation is noticing when your mind has taken a different direction and bringing it back to focus. Without judgement. It does take patience. Not only to bring the mind back to focus again, and again, and again, but also to take time every day, even if it's just for a minute, to tune in and quieten your mind. Regular practice has huge benefits for general well-being. In today's society of stress, business and drama, taking time to be still is more important than ever. Looking after your mental well-being, as with all exercise, is a lifelong practice.

Perhaps your goal is to be a little more mindful in everyday life. Or to take a few minutes each morning to breathe with more awareness. Or you may enjoy more formal practice such as specific Buddhist or yogic meditation. There is a meditation practice out there for everybody! It does not matter if you are looking for a way to balance your emotions, or you are a spiritual person hoping to deepen your connection to that which is greater than us. Everyone and anyone can experience the benefits of meditation, no matter the paths that leads you to it.

Meditation is, all at once, the simplest thing and the hardest thing. It is a letting go and surrendering, but also can be a connecting and a union to something else – magic? Goddess? The Otherworld? Universal consciousness? Spirit? It can be different for everyone, and different every time you meditate.

As we peel away, or let fall, the layers of fear, anxiety, stress, consumerism and pressure, we may come to our true selves.

Perhaps from this place of freedom, we may travel to other realms or visualise our own success, seek connections or wisdom. Maybe we find for ourselves, within ourselves, forgiveness, love and compassion. I truly hope so.

Thank you for joining me on this journey, and may your ongoing journey be joyful and full of learning. I hope you will return to the meditations in this book that spoke to you or inspired you and share them with others, read them aloud, record them, spread the magic of meditation however you wish.

About the Author

Sarah Robinson is a yoga teacher and author based in Bath, UK (once named after a goddess: the ancient Roman town of *Aquae Sulis*). Her background is in science; she holds an MSc Psychology & Neuroscience and has studied at Bath, Exeter and Harvard University. She loves exploring the power of myth, magic and story in both her writing and yoga teaching, and is passionate about helping everyone connect to their own special magic and inner power.

She has three books published previously by Womancraft Publishing; *Yoga for Witches*, *Yin Magic* and *Kitchen Witch*.

Find Sarah online:
  Website: sentiayoga.com
  Instagram: @Yogaforwitches

Resources

This is not an exhaustive list by any means, but a few ideas if you are keen to learn more about meditation, mindfulness, intuition, and intention.

My books that explore meditation and yoga

Yoga for Witches by Sarah Robinson

Yin Magic by Sarah Robinson

A few of my favourites

Buddha's Brain: The Practical Neuroscience of Happiness, Love, And Wisdom by Rick Hanson

Intuitive Witchcraft: How to Use Intuition to Elevate Your Craft by Astrea Taylor

Psychic Witch: A Metaphysical Guide to Meditation, Magick and Manifestation by Mat Auryn

Wild & Wise: Sacred Feminine Meditations for Women's Circles and Personal Awakening by Amy Bammel Wilding

Self-Compassion: The Proven Power of Being Kind to Yourself by Kristin Neff

About the Artist

Izumi Omori utilises her Japanese artistic and other cultural influences as she explores, absorbs, and interprets Earth's nature around her, wherever she may find herself in this world.

Born at the foot of Mt Fuji in 1967, Izumi started painting at the age of three, and she has grown up with an intense love for the spectacle that nature so willingly offers. Like the pure water of the sacred mountain waterfalls, lakes, and rivers near her home town of Kofu, her passion to express the love of her surroundings within her art runs deep and vibrant in an enthusiastic colour of learning.

Izumi's work features the magic, power, and miracles of our planet's nature and beauty. Her paintings shimmer with light and living energy, capturing transitory moments of multifaceted life and growth, within layers of paint and texture. They have both strength and delicacy, a blending of the most powerful natural elements, along with Japanese style and sensitivity.

About Womancraft

Womancraft Publishing was founded on the revo-
lutionary vision that women and words can change
the world. We act as midwife to transformational
women's words that have the power to challenge,
inspire, heal and speak to the silenced aspects of
ourselves.

We believe that:

○ books are a fabulous way of transmitting
powerful transformation,

○ values should be juicy actions, lived out,

○ ethical business is a key way to
contribute to conscious change.

At the heart of our Womancraft philosophy is fairness and
integrity. Creatives and women have always been underpaid.
Not on our watch! We split royalties 50:50 with our authors.
We work on a full circle model of giving and receiving: reaching backwards, supporting TreeSisters' reforestation projects,
and forwards via Worldreader, providing books at no cost to
education projects for girls and women.

We are proud that Womancraft is walking its talk and engaging so many women each year via our books and online. Join

the revolution! Sign up to the mailing list at womancraftpub-lishing.com and find us on social media for exclusive offers:

womancraftpublishing

womancraft_publishing

womancraftpublishing.com/books

Use of Womancraft Work

Often women contact us asking if and how they may use our work. We love seeing our work out in the world. We love you sharing our words further. And we ask that you respect our hard work by acknowledging the source of the words.

We are delighted for short quotes from our books – up to 200 words – to be shared as memes or in your own articles or books, provided they are clearly accompanied by the author's name and the book's title.

We are also very happy for the materials in our books to be shared amongst women's communities: to be studied by book groups, discussed in classes, read from in ceremony, quoted on social media…with the following provisos:

- If content from the book is shared in written or spoken form, the book's author and title must be referenced clearly.

- The only person fully qualified to teach the material from any of our titles is the author of the book itself. There are no accredited teachers of this work. Please do not make claims of this sort.

○ If you are creating a course devoted to the content of one of our books, its title and author must be clearly acknowledged on all promotional material (posters, websites, social media posts).

○ The book's cover may be used in promotional materials or social media posts. The cover art is copyright of the artist and has been licensed exclusively for this book. Any element of the book's cover or font may not be used in branding your own marketing materials when teaching the content of the book, or content very similar to the original book.

○ No more than two double page spreads, or four single pages of any book may be photocopied as teaching materials.

We are delighted to offer a 20% discount of over five copies going to one address. You can order these on our webshop, or email us. If you require further clarification, email us at: info@womancraftpublishing.com

Yoga for Witches

Sarah Robinson

Yoga for Witches explores a new kind of journey, connecting two powerful spiritual disciplines, with enchanting effects! Witchcraft and yoga share many similarities that are explored in combination, in this groundbreaking new title from Sarah Robinson, certified yoga instructor and experienced witch.

Yoga for Witches shares exercises, poses and the knowledge you need to connect to your own special magic and inner power.

○ Explore how ancient yogis sought out magic.

○ Weave magic through spells, mantra, meditation and yoga practice.

○ Discover some of the goddesses and gods of yogic and witch culture.

○ Connect to the power of the sun, moon and earth via witchcraft and yoga.

○ Explore the magic of the chakras.

Namaste, Witches!

Yin Magic

Sarah Robinson

Yin Magic: How to be Still shows how ancient Chinese Taoist alchemical practices can mingle with yoga and magic to enhance our well-being from sleep to stress-levels, helping us to move beyond burnout cycles and embody the beauty of letting go. It shares:

- ○ What yin is…and why it matters.

- ○ An introduction to the practice of yin yoga

- ○ Yin yoga journeys for each season and the meridians.

- ○ Insight from cutting-edge neuroscience research.

- ○ Connections between Celtic, witch and Chinese medicine traditions.

- ○ Sympathetic magic and how to bring it into your yoga practice.

- ○ How to embrace the magic in the darker times of night, new moon and winter.

Yin Magic helps us to make everyday magic at a sumptuously slow pace as an antidote to the busyness of modern life.

Wild & Wise: sacred feminine meditations for women's circles and personal awakening

Amy Bammel Wilding

The stunning debut by Amy Bammel Wilding is not merely a collection of guided meditations, but a potent tool for personal and global transformation. The meditations beckon you to explore the powerful realm of symbolism and archetypes, inviting you to access your wild and wise inner knowing.

Cycles of Belonging: Honouring ourselves through the sacred cycles of life

Stella Tomlinson

A guide to unlocking the powers of cyclic living to lead a more fulfilling, meaningful, and wholehearted life. *Cycles of Belonging* offers an embodied feminine and feminist psycho-spiritual path for women to reclaim their inner wisdom, follow the callings of their soul, and come home to a profound sense of belonging to the seasons and cycles of life.

Walking with Persephone

Molly Remer

Midlife can be a time of great change – inner and outer: a time of letting go of the old, burnout and disillusionment. But how do we journey through this? And what can we learn in the process? Molly Remer is our personal guide to the unraveling and reweaving required in midlife. She invites you to take a walk with the goddess Persephone, whose story of descent into the underworld has much to teach us.

Red Tents: Unravelling our Past and Weaving a Shared Future

Mary Ann Clements and Aisha Hannibal

Red Tents weaves together the voices and experiences of many women to create a shared story about the role Red Tents can play in our lives. We document our shared hope, vision and dream – Red Tents as liberatory community spaces for women around the world.

Full of inspiration and practical learning, along with questions and practices to support and stimulate discussion about some of the challenges Red Tents face. *Red Tents* is written by the founders of the Red Tent Directory, including interviews with over seventy women from diverse backgrounds who run Red Tents.

Made in United States
Orlando, FL
20 August 2023